THE WAY
IT WAS
in the SOUTH

THE WAY IT WAS

in the SOUTH

Clarence P. Hornung

SMITHMARK

This edition published in 1992 by SMITHMARK Publishers, Inc.
16 East 32nd Street, New York, NY 10016

Printed by special arrangement with
William S. Konecky Associates, Inc.

SMITHMARK books are available for bulk purchase for
sales promotion and premium use. For details write
or telephone the Manager of Special Sales, SMITHMARK
Publishers, Inc., 16 East 32nd Street, New York, NY 10016.
(212) 532-6600.

ISBN 0-8317-9358-9

Printed in the United States of America

CONTENTS

THE SOUTH

The Old Dominion
& the Carolinas

THE JAMES, ABOVE RICHMOND . . .

RAPIDS ON THE JAMES . . .CANAL

SCENE . . .PANORAMIC VIEW OF

RICHMOND . . .NATURAL BRIDGE

. . . HARPERS FERRY PETERSBURG

GAP . . . THE FRENCH BROAD . . .

MOUNTAIN ISLAND . . . WILMINGTON

. . . STATE HOUSE, RALEIGH . . .

. . . PICKING COTTON . . .CHARLESTON

. . . DOCK SCENES . . . BATTERY

PROMENADE . . . CHARLESTON HOTEL . . .

MAGNOLIA GARDENS . . . CUSTOMS HOUSE

. . . MILLS HOUSE

The Old Dominion & the Carolinas

THE JAMES, ABOVE RICHMOND

"I have been planing what I would shew you: a flower here, a tree there ... on this side a hill, on that a river. Indeed, madam, I know nothing so charming as our own country"—

Thomas Jefferson

THE "OLD DOMINION" HAS PROfoundly touched us in a way quite unlike any other region. Like its western ridges, the spine of the Appalachian range that divides the coast from the prairie, Virginia and the Carolinas contains an enigma that fires the imagination and that changed the nation's history.

Coastal settlement began early, at Jamestown in 1607. Extending throughout Virginia and the Carolinas, the coastal plain rises gently from the Tidewater Basin in Virginia to the rolling foothills at the base of the Appalachians. These foothills, known as the Piedmont plateau, run down through the Carolinas. Under British rule the area developed quickly. Tobacco and indigo were the main crops and enjoyed a bounty. By the time of the Revolution the area was thickly settled. The increasing scarcity of land gradually pushed settlers westward. As they reached the Blue Ridge, Allegheny, and Great Smoky mountains a distinct difference arose. The mountainous terrain made larger plantations impractical. The land necessitated smaller, more self-sufficient farms on tracts of about a hundred acres. The rugged character of the land gave rise to a political division that would forever separate the mountain people from the Piedmont and its political control.

The mountain people lived in a situation that was far removed from the "genteel" elegance of Richmond or Charleston. They developed their own culture, techniques of curing meat, and handicrafts to fit the unique conditions of their lives. Like the sounds they teased out of a dulcimer or fiddle, the mountain people created a pleasing though primitive world whose basis was simplicity itself.

In contrast, the bustling seaports of Wilmington in North Carolina, and Charleston in South Carolina, were vital in a Southern economy that was buoyant on the cotton trade. During the "war for secession" both ports became havens for rakish blockade runners who traded cotton for munitions. The center of rebellious spirit, Charleston did not surrender Fort Sumter in its harbor until February of 1865. Four years earlier the Civil War began when General Beauregard opened fire on federal forces stationed there.

Mansions like Shirley and Westover on the James River and other proud old buildings cast shadows that hold riddles and secrets. The Tredegar Iron Works in Richmond and houses that stood witness to battles like Chancellorsville and Manassas—all have tales to tell. Deep within Monticello and Mount Vernon or the painstaking restoration of colonial Williamsburg, both questions and answers await. These shadows have seen all the dreams come and pass by: the Confederate States of America, a crumbling dream that hung on like a wildflower clinging to the jagged ridgeline of Old Rag mountain; the bittersweet dream of the Cherokee nation that died on the "Trail of Tears"; liberty, the burning dream in the eyes of Patrick Henry, Thomas Jefferson, and George Washington. These hammer relentlessly like the surf pounding the shore at Cape Hatteras. While the muddy James River turns the Atlantic brown at Hampton Roads and John Brown's ghost stalks Harpers Ferry, the enigmatic fire that springs from this pastoral land remains.

How is it that rebellion is spawned in a place such as this? The iron fences of Charleston and the sun-bleached tobacco drying barns of the Piedmont attest to a paradox. Mountains ripping four thousand feet out of soft hills. Dunes of fine sand drifting in ocean breezes on the Outer Banks. Rivers like the James, Potomac, and Rappahannack that flow serenely through green hills. Virginia and the Carolinas embody thousands of striking contrasts. The Blue Ridge and Allegheny mountains as they rise creating the Shenandoah valley. The defiant battery at Charleston jutting out toward the Atlantic. The squalor of the tenant farmer. The aristocratic elegance of the plantation houses.

One of the greatest riddles that remains unsolved concerns the "lost colony" on Roanoke Island—located in the region safely protected from Carolina's Outer Banks and the seventy-mile strip of reef above Cape Hatteras—where an English colony vanished. In 1585 Raleigh sent out his first group to the domain he called "Virginia." This colony left for England after enduring many hardships, on Sir Francis Drake's fleet. Only a few days after their departure Sir Richard Grenville arrived with fresh provisions and more colonists. Of the original colony none was found alive, and the only trace of its existence was the word "Croatan" carved on a tree. Virginia Dare, the first white child born in America, was the granddaughter of John White, the leader of this new group of colonists.

There are further mysteries that defy solution, like the "bald spots" in the Blue Ridge Mountains. These are all elements comprising the enigmatic character of the "Old Dominion" and the Carolinas. The striking beauty of these contrasts has inspired and drawn the respect of many who built this nation. A middle-aged major, speaking to a class of cadets at Virginia Military Institute before the outbreak of the Civil War put it this way: "The time may be near when your state needs your services, but it has not yet come. If that time comes then draw your swords and throw away the scabbards." History would know Major Thomas Jackson better as "Stonewall." He, and others like him, born in this land of striking beauty, would forever change the face of our nation.

Because of its importance, Richmond—Virginia's proud capital, and capital of the Confederacy—suffered the ravages of war as did few other cities

Very few cities in America can compare with Richmond, a stately rectilinear town, for concentration of historical allusion. It has celebrated monuments to Lee, Jefferson Davis (for Richmond was the second capital of the Confederacy), and Stonewall Jackson; General Lee's home, now the headquarters of the Virginia Historical Society, is here, and so is that of Edgar Allan Poe. But what I liked best, next to the incomparable executive mansion, is the heroic (and heroically ugly) equestrian statue of George Washington, which was cast in Munich of all places, and which now stands in Capitol Square. The general's eyes look sternly at the state house and his finger, like a flail, points to the penitentiary! Richmond is not a very large city, but it has great wealth; most of the modern fortunes come from tobacco. It is heavily industrialized, and is the biggest cigarette manufacturing center in the world. Tobacco is a small man's crop; the average holding in the American South is about three acres. In Virginia and western North Carolina most growers are owners; in Georgia they are mostly tenants. There are no great tobacco "plantations" like cotton plantations.

JOHN GUNTHER
Inside U.S.A., 1947

SCENE ON THE CANAL

RICHMOND, FROM THE DRIVE OVERLOOKING THE CITY

Richmond's broad streets and drives are starred with buildings and monuments of historic note: the fine executive mansion, state capitol and monuments to Washington, Lee, and Davis

RICHMOND FROM HOLLYWOOD

The point from which the most commanding and comprehensive view of Richmond is visible, bears the name of Hollywood Cemetery, a picturesque elevation in the north-western suburbs, where rest the remains of many illustrious men, and of thousands who in the recent struggle "Went down to their graves in bloody shrouds." The scene from President's Hill, in Hollywood, is one that never tires the eye, because it embraces a picture which somewhere among its lights and shadows presents features that constantly appeal to imagination and refined taste. In the great perspective which bounds the horizon the distant hills and forests take new color from the changing clouds; while nearer—almost at your feet—the James River, brawling over the rocks, and chanting its perpetual requiem to the dead who lie around, catches from the sunshine playing on its ruffled breast kaleidoscopic hues. Intermediate in elevation between the river and the summit of President's Hill winds, in a graceful curve, the canal, seeking its basin at the town; and not far away are the forges of the Tredegar Iron-works, the fiery chimneys of which at night belch forth flames that send their sparkle into a thousand windows, and make pictures in the rippling waters.

J. R. THOMPSON
Picturesque America, 1872

*Towering 215 feet above Cedar Creek, the limestone arch—
called the Natural Bridge—is one of Virginia's unique
wonders, characterized by many as a ''freak of nature''...*

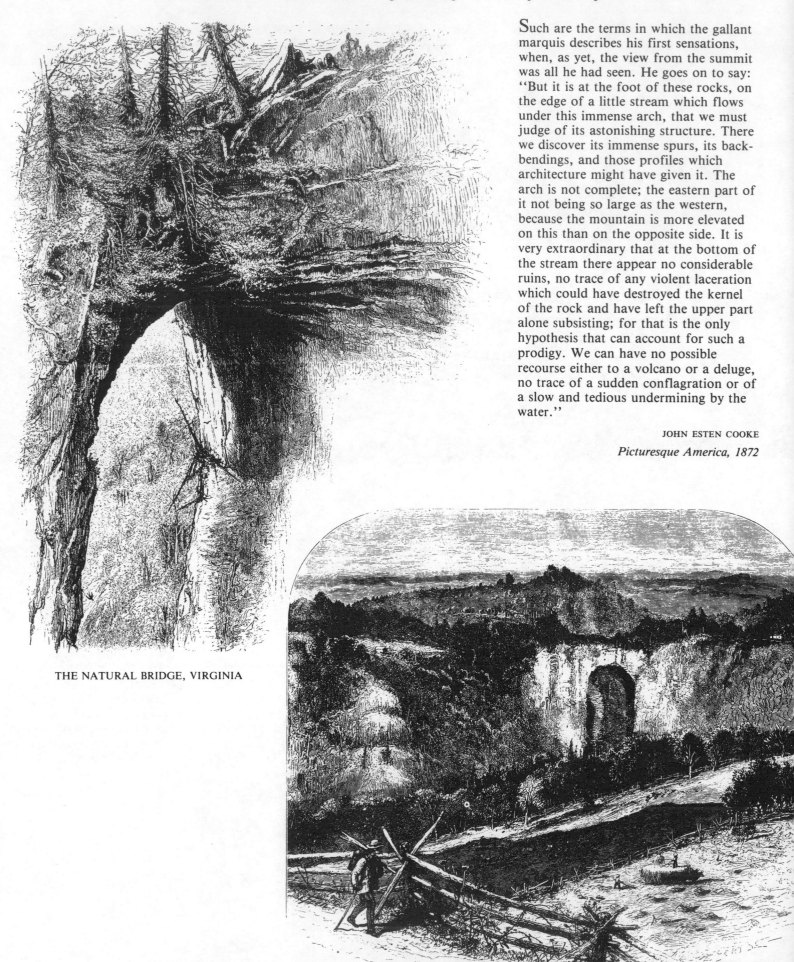

Such are the terms in which the gallant marquis describes his first sensations, when, as yet, the view from the summit was all he had seen. He goes on to say: ''But it is at the foot of these rocks, on the edge of a little stream which flows under this immense arch, that we must judge of its astonishing structure. There we discover its immense spurs, its back-bendings, and those profiles which architecture might have given it. The arch is not complete; the eastern part of it not being so large as the western, because the mountain is more elevated on this than on the opposite side. It is very extraordinary that at the bottom of the stream there appear no considerable ruins, no trace of any violent laceration which could have destroyed the kernel of the rock and have left the upper part alone subsisting; for that is the only hypothesis that can account for such a prodigy. We can have no possible recourse either to a volcano or a deluge, no trace of a sudden conflagration or of a slow and tedious undermining by the water.''

JOHN ESTEN COOKE
Picturesque America, 1872

THE NATURAL BRIDGE, VIRGINIA

THE NATURAL BRIDGE AND ITS SURROUNDINGS

. . . shaped and eroded by the stream below—a sublime and rugged formation—visited by Washington and Jefferson, whose accounts spurred thousands to view the spectacle

UNDER THE NATURAL BRIDGE

The whole arch seems to be formed of one and the same stone; for the joints which one remarks are the effect of lightning, which struck this part in 1779. The other head has not the smallest vein, and the intrados is so smooth that the martins, which fly around it in great numbers, cannot fasten on it. The abutments, which have a gentle slope, are entire, and, without being absolute planes, have all the polish which a current of water would give to unhewn stone in a certain time. The four rocks adjacent to the abutments seem to be perfectly homogeneous, and to have a very trifling slope. The two rocks on the right bank of the rivulet are two hundred feet high above the surface of the water, the intrados of the arch a hundred and fifty, and the two rocks on the left bank a hundred and eighty. If we consider this bridge simply as a picturesque object, we are struck with the majesty with which it towers in the valley. The white-oaks which grow upon it seem to rear their lofty summits to the clouds, while the same trees which border on the rivulet appear like shrubs.

MARQUIS DE CHASTELLUX, 1781

Picturesque America, 1872

Where the Shenandoah flows into the Potomac—and three states meet—on the extreme edge of West Virginia's eastern border, is Harpers Ferry, famed in pre-Civil War days

After Brown made his historic raid on Harpers Ferry, he was captured by Colonel Robert E. Lee and Lieutenant "Jeb" Stuart of the United States Army. He was tried, convicted, and hanged for murder, for inciting slaves to revolt, and for treason. Before being put to death, he told his inquisitors, " . . . I pity the poor in bondage that have none to help them; that is why I am here; not to gratify any personal animosity, revenge or vindictive spirit. It is my sympathy with the oppressed and the wronged, that are as good as you and as precious in the sight of God . . . I wish to say, furthermore, that you had better—all you people at the South— prepare yourselves for a settlement of that question that must come up for settlement sooner than you are prepared for it. You may dispose of me very easily. I am nearly disposed of now; but this question is still to be settled—this negro question I mean; the end of that is not yet . . . "

JOHN BROWN
*Before his death
December 2, 1859*

HARPERS FERRY

PETERSBURG GAP

*Here, the abolitionist John Brown and his followers
captured the federal arsenal for which Brown was hanged,
though many sympathized, regarding him as a martyr*

MARYLAND ROAD

A hundred miles away in an arrow-line
Lies the other defended king of the giant
   chess,
Broad streeted Richmond...
The trees in the streets are old trees used
   to living with people,
Family-trees that remember your grand-
   father's name.
It is still a clan-city, a family-city, a city
That thinks of the war, on the whole, as
   a family matter...

                STEPHEN VINCENT BENET
                John Brown's Body, 1927

This spot, so celebrated for its wild and majestic scenery, is in Jefferson County, at the confluence of Shenandoah and Potomac Rivers, where, after the union of their waters, they find a passage through the rocky barrier of the Blue Ridge, twelve hundred feet in height. Mr. Jefferson, in his *"Notes on Virginia,"* has given a full and graphic account of the scene, which he characterizes as "one of the most stupendous in nature." "Jefferson's Rock," the spot where it is said Mr. Jefferson wrote the description, is a pile of huge, detached rocks, leaning over the precipitous cliffs of the Shenandoah, and looking into the mountain gorge of the Potomac...There is also a most enchanting prospect obtained from the summit of a mountain opposite, about a mile and a half farther up, on the Maryland side of the river. The eye here reaches a very wide extent of country, fields, woodlands, and plantations; while the Shenandoah, as it is traceable upon the magic picture, appears like a series of beautiful lakes.

            Gleason's Pictorial
            July 29, 1854

MARYLAND HEIGHTS

Along the western fringes of North Carolina, the French Broad winds its way between ragged escarpments of the Blue Ridge and the Great Smokies . . .

Still another section of the country which seems destined at no distant day to become a place of recreation, and to attract the artist and lover of Nature, is that portion of Western North Carolina through which course the beautiful waters of the French Broad River and other mountain-streams, and which may be described in general terms as the table-land of the Blue Ridge. The fame of the beauty and the sublimity of the scenery is extensive, and the realization does not belie the report. Tall, grim, old rocks lift their bald heads far, far toward the heavens, in all the sublimity of solemn grandeur; while in the vision of the distant lowlands, that may be enjoyed from this summit or that, is a soft, sweet delicacy which breathes almost of the celestial, and makes one feel unconscious of aught save the panorama of loveliness before him. Indeed, it would seem as if Nature had selected this region for the display of her fantastic power in uplifting the earth, and giving to it strange shapes and startling contrasts—in imparting curious physiognomies to the mountains and evoking melody from the water-falls.

F. G. DE FONTAINE
Picturesque America, 1872

FERRY ON THE FRENCH BROAD

MOUNTAIN ISLAND

. . . its course cutting through rugged terrain, giving way to rocky canyons and mountainous ravines of singular beauty

THE FRENCH BROAD

And how fair is this same forest in late autumn...The damp earth is elastic under your feet; the high blades of grass do not stir; long threads lie shining on the blanched turf, white with dew. You breathe tranquilly; but there is a strange tremor in the soul. You walk along the forest's edge, look after your dog, and meanwhile loved forms, loved faces dead and living, come to your mind; long, long, slumbering impressions unexpectedly awaken; the fancy darts off and soars like a bird; and all moves so clearly and stands out before your eyes. The heart at one time throbs and beats, plunging passionately forward; at another it is drowned beyond recall in memories. Your whole life, as it were, unrolls lightly and rapidly before you: a man at such times possesses all his past, all his feelings and his powers—all his soul; and there is nothing around to hinder him—no sun, no wind, no sound...

IVAN TURGENEV

A Sportsman's Sketches, 1852

May I be dead when all the woods are old,
And shaped to patterns of the planners' minds,
When great unnatural rows of trees unfold
Their tender foliage to the April winds,
May I be dead when Sandy is not free,
And transferred to a channel not its own,
Water through years that sang for her and me.
Over the precipice and soft sandstone...
Let wild rose be an epitaph for me
When redbirds go and helpless sike pokes must,
And red beans on the honey-locust tree
Are long-forgotten banners turned to dust...
I weep to think these hills where I awoke.
Saw God's great beauty, wonderful and strange,
Will be destroyed, stem and flower and oak,
And I would rather die than see the change.

JESSE STUART

May I be Dead

"THE LOVERS' LEAP"

When Wilmington—once the state's leading port—on the Cape Fear River, fell to the North, blockade runners were cut off, and the end of the war for the South was in sight

TURPENTINE DISTILLERY, WILMINGTON

MARKET STREET, WILMINGTON

*In 1792, Raleigh—the newly chosen capital city—
was carved out of the wilderness, its architects
accused of building "a city of streets without houses"*

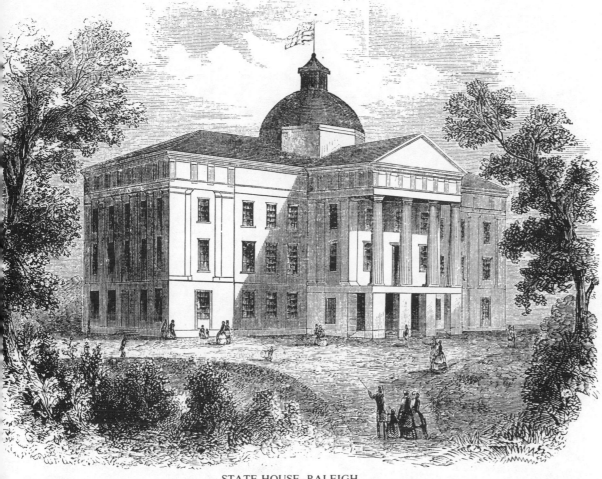

STATE HOUSE, RALEIGH

CAPE FEAR BANK, WILMINGTON

Roanoke Island is the well-known setting, with the smell of red honeysuckle and partridge-berry blossoms filling the air, of Paul Green's *The Lost Colony;* and despite the passage of years, it still has the power to move audiences to wonder at the disappearance of the early colonists into the wilderness. Blackbeard's ghost, romantics say, still haunts Ocrakoke Island, where wild ponies once ran free. From Oregon Inlet to Ocrakoke the sea, sand, and beach grass in their unspoiled state provide a lonely, contemplative setting. The Great Dismal Swamp, at the upper edge of North Carolina's coast plain and spilling over into Virginia, is still largely inaccessible. A spongy quagmire of cypress, black gum, and juniper that filter out the sunlight, it is truly the "region of unearthly darkness lying across sunlit land" that Pierce describes, one of the still secret places of the American terrain. But it is western North Carolina— across the Piedmont and in the powerful presence of the ragged escarpment of the Blue Ridge—that really captures one.

ARNOLD EHRLICH, ED.
The Beautiful Country

Decades before the Civil War the production, shipping, and marketing of cotton dominated every aspect of Southern life, its culture and economy . . .

The plantation system throughout most of the southern states was almost equally divided between the larger estates, held by those descended from the colonial aristocracy— Washington's type as well as his kinsmen, the Lees; the old Hugenot families of South Carolina; wealthy planters of French creoles of Louisiana—and smaller planters who owned no more than one or a dozen slaves. Of this group, poorly equipped with clumsy hoes and mule-drawn plows, slaves were often beaten by "drivers," assigned to discipline the laggards by flogging at night, after the day's labors ended. These little "one horse plantations" were described by Mark Twain: "A rail fence around a two-acre yard . . .big double log house for the white folks— hewed logs, with the chinks stopped up with mud or mortar, and these mud-stripes had been white-washed some time or another; round-log kitchen, with a big, broad, open but roofed passage joining it to the house; log smoke-house back of the kitchen; three little log nigger-cabins in a rot t'other side the smoke-house . . . outside of the fence a garden and a water-melon patch; then the cotton fields begin; and after the fields, the woods."

MARK TWAIN
Huckleberry Finn, 1884

WHIPPING COTTON.

PICKIN[G]

MOTING COTTON

SHIP[PING]

GINNING COTTON BY STEAM

GROWING, PROCESSING AND SHIPPING   THE COTTON CROP, SEA ISLANDS, PORT ROYAL, S.C.

. . . as the demand from abroad, for cash crops, encouraged the development of the plantation system, where land was rich and productive, manned by the cheapest human labor

PLANTING COTTON.

HOEING COTTON.

PACKING COTTON.

Planters, particularly native planters, have a kind of affection for their Negroes, incredible to those who have not observed its effects. If rebellious they punish them—if well behaved, they not infrequently reward them. In health they treat them with uniform kindness, in sickness with attention and sympathy. I once called on a native planter—a young bachelor, like many of his class, who had graduated at Cambridge and traveled in Europe—yet Northern education and foreign habits did not destroy the Mississippian. I found him by the bedside of a dying slave, nursing him with a kindness of voice and manner, and displaying a manly sympathy with his sufferings, honorable to himself and to humanity. On large plantations hospitals are erected for the reception of the sick, and the best medical attendance is provided for them. The physicians of Natchez derive a large proportion of their incomes from attending plantations. On some estates a physician permanently resides, whose time may be supposed sufficiently taken up in attending to the health of from one to two hundred persons. Often several plantations, if the force on each is small, unite and employ one physician for the whole.

JOSEPH HOLT INGRAHAM
South-West, 1835

The first impression the streets of Charleston give is that of retiring respectability. There are no splendid avenues, no imposing public structures; but a few fine old churches and many noble private mansions standing in a sort of dingy stateliness amid their embowering magnolias, command our attention. Our New York custom, derived from our Dutch ancestors, of painting our brick fronts, is not in vogue here, where the houses have the sombre but rich toning that age alone can give when its slow pencillings are never disturbed by the rude intrusion of the painter's brush. The Charleston mansions are nearly always built with the gable-end to the street. At one side rises a tier of open verandas, into the lower of which the main entrance to the building is placed. Usually, after the English fashion, a high brick wall encloses the grounds of the house, and it is only through an open gate-way that one catches a glimpse of flowers, and shrubs, and vines, that bloom and expand within the enclosure. But the rich dark green of the magnolia half screens the unsmoothed brick walls far above, and seems to hold the ancient structure in the hush of venerable repose.

O.B. BUNCE

Picturesque America, 1872

LOADING COTTON, CHARLESTON

A COTTON WHARF, CHARLESTON

. . . yet on quiet city streets and squares of this "American Venice," the languid serenity of the Southern tempo was in sharp contrast with dockside activity

CHARLESTON AND BAY, FROM ST. MICHAEL'S CHURCH

So much has been written of Charleston, and Charlestonians are so touchy, that you sometimes wonder what to say. Still, there is one very evident thing about Charleston: it is the most glamorous city in America, a city with an antique grace so discreetly guarded it makes one think of heirlooms in daily use, a city that has blessedly escaped both the bulldozers and the ministrations of antiquarian wealth. Its colonial aspect seems less glamorous, however, than its fame for Castilian pride of birth. Old Charlestonians are admittedly complacent, but less remote often than the families of softdrink barons with villas at Myrtle Beach. Content with their own company, they can and do receive cordially; and sometimes they even mix their blue blood in marriage with outlander red. But the myth seduces. Most Americans are homesick for lords and ladies; they like to think that somewhere lofty beings fit their ideal of nobility. So what is Charleston more famous for than the St. Celia Society, the ball-giving social fortress which legend erects to Trojan heights of impregnability? The myth is implicit in these doggerel lines:

> *In Boston the Lodges*
> *   speak to the Cabots*
> *And the Cabots speak only*
> *   to God;*
> *In Charleston the Pinck-*
> *   neys speak to the Rhetts*
> *And the Rhetts don't*
> *   bother about God.*

WILLIAM FRANCIS GUESS

South Carolina, 1947

Visitors from the North came to enjoy the cool delights of Charleston's balmy climate—to promenade on the Battery—to partake of its "different" atmosphere

CHARLESTON, FROM THE BAY

Charleston is in fact a gem; it is also a kind of mummy, like Savannah. I heard one unkind friend nickname it "Death on the Atlantic," and call it "a perfect example of what the South must never be again." Be this as it may, it belongs in that strange eclectic category of American "sights" not to be missed, practically like the Taos Pueblo and Niagara Falls. Once it was the fourth biggest city in America, and probably the most brilliantly sophisticated; today much of its polish has worn off, though it still retains a cardinal quality of grace. Also, a city on a narrow island between two small rivers, it has great local pride. "Charleston, sir," one of the local worthies once told a Yankee interloper, "is that untarnished jewel shining regally at that sacred spot where the Ashley and the Cooper join their majestic waters to form the Atlantic Ocean." Once Charleston was known as "Capital of the Plantation;" but it is a seaport, and so has been vulnerable to the incursions of the foreign-born. The leading commercial family today derives from a group of six Sicilian brothers, who own theaters, hotels, automobile agencies, and the like; there are also Chinese, Greek, Portuguese, and Sephardic Jewish communities. Many of the great old houses are, one by one, being sold or boarded up. Some were used during the war by the Army and Navy (Charleston played an active and honorable role in war activities); some, leased by northern owners, are empty most of the year; in some the last entrenched survivors of the old society—in the main wealthy widows who inherited fortunes made on rice—still hold out.

JOHN GUNTHER
Inside U.S.A., 1947

EAST BATTERY, PROMENADE

"In no part of America," noted Morse in his American Geography, *"are the social blessings enjoyed more rationally and liberally than in Charleston"*

CHARLESTON HOTEL

A CHARLESTON GARDEN

MAGNOLIAS

BAY STREET, CHARLESTON

Shipments are no longer raw cotton by the bale, but finished cotton by the bolt, woven in the large number of textile plants in the Charleston area

The town was Charleston and on their city homes the rice aristocracy lavished wealth from their swamps. In urban retreat they lived out the summer season, giving themselves "every pleasure and convenience to which their warmer climate and better circumstances invite them." The city itself seemed unpleasantly exotic to some visitors. Picturesque houses built to suit the climate and the polyglot background of the people broke too many rules of proportion and academic form. "In Charleston persons vie with one another, not who shall have the finest, but who the coolest house," wrote La Rochefoucauld-Liancourt. The aristocratic nature of the city's social life was maintained long after wealth had shifted to new sections, and in a region of few cities its preeminence was indisputable.

MARSHALL B. DAVIDSON

Life in America, 1951

NEW CUSTOM HOUSE, CHARLESTON

MILLS HOUSE, CHARLESTON

From the Savannah...
to the Suwannee River

THE SAVANNAH . . . AUGUSTA . . .

TEXTILE MILL . . . COTTON BOATS . . .

FORSYTH PARK, SAVANNAH . . . VIEW

OF THE HARBOR . . . BULL STREET . . .

GEORGIA VILLAGE MARKETPLACE . . .

ATHENS . . . ROME . . . ATLANTA . . .

THE CAPITOL . . . ATLANTA BUILDINGS

. . .RESIDENCES . . . ST. JOHN'S RIVER

. . . GREEN COVE SPRINGS . . .

THE OCKLAWAHA . . . ST. AUGUSTINE

. . .ST. MARK'S CASTLE . . . CITY GATE

. . . THE EVERGLADES . . . LAKE

OKEECHOBEE . . . PENSACOLA

THE SAVANNAH

From the Savannah...
to the Suwannee River

A JOURNEY BEYOND THE BANKS OF THE Savannah River into Georgia and the heart of the Old South begins where the river meets the sea, at Georgia's oldest city and first capital, Savannah. Here, in an area of magnolia, pine, and live oak, settlers led by James Oglethorpe landed in 1733. From this point, settlement began to move slowly west and south into Georgia's southern coastal and Piedmont areas and into Florida.

The Savannah River was already carrying traffic at the time Oglethorpe and his party reached the coast. Augusta, up the river from Savananah, had been a trading post since 1717. After the American Revolution it boomed, and by 1820 it had become an important terminus for riverboats, wagon trains, and traders, moving produce from the interior to the sea.

Augusta and Savannah are among Georgia's oldest cities, and as settlers moved west into the interior to establish plantations in the fertile red-dirt valleys, these towns became the political, cultural, and commercial centers of Georgia's rich agricultural empire. Tobacco and cotton moved through these cities on their way to other American and European ports, and the secession issue, first from the Crown and then from the Union, was debated there by Georgia's statesmen and journalists.

Atlanta, Georgia's capital since 1868, and now the busy industrial and commercial center of the New South, is a relatively new town compared to Augusta and Savannah. Hardy Ivy, Atlanta's first settler, built his cabin there near the Appalachian foothills only in 1833. In 1837, Terminus, an end-of-the-line railroad town, was founded there. Incorporated in 1843 as Marthasville, it was renamed Atlanta in 1845. By then it was a major railroad and marketing hub, and it became a vital commercial and supply center for the Confederacy during the Civil War.

Beyond the cities, where the merchants built magnificent homes and laid out manicured gardens, stretched the real heart of Georgia— the hills, woods, marshes, and flatlands in which the great majority of its citizens lived well into the present century. Here lumber was cut from the great pine forests; marble, clay, and iron were dug from the earth; and tobacco and cotton were planted and harvested in mile after mile of fertile field.

Georgia's wealth came from the land, and especially from cotton. Aided by the cotton gin, and by an abundance of slaves, the wealth of Georgia's planter class was prodigious. The legendary and languid life of the Old South flourished here for almost three-quarters of a century, until bitter disputes with the industrial North led to secession and war. Georgia became first a supply center and then a battleground: in 1864 Union troops under W. T. Sherman entered Atlanta, burned it to the ground, and began a march to the sea, during which they plundered and burned everything for fifty miles along their path.

In the southeastern tip of Georgia lies the great Okefenokee Swamp, where the Suwannee River has its source. The Suwannee—immortalized by Stephen Foster, who never saw it, and could not spell its name—flows along moss-lined banks, through pine and oak forests, in a land that closely resembles much of Georgia. Towns in this region were always small, and though a plantation economy developed here based on cotton and sugar, it never grew to a scale to match Georgia's.

A Spanish possession until 1819, Florida was settled chiefly by missionaries, explorers, traders—not farmers. In a hilly agricultural area in the middle of Florida's northern section stands Tallahassee, Florida's capital. Situated among lakes, springs, forests, and lush, tropical gardens, Tallahassee successfully repulsed Union attacks in the last months of the war, and retains many antebellum homes.

To the south, along Florida's Atlantic coast, is St. Augustine, the oldest city in America, founded by Europeans. It was established in 1565 on a peninsula between the Matanzas and San Sebastian rivers, near the site where Ponce de Leon landed in 1513 in his search for the fountain of youth. South and west of St. Augustine is Florida's agricultural region, now growing one of America's largest citrus crops, the first seeds of which were brought to Florida from Spain by de Leon. Farther south is the area dominated by Lake Okeechobee, the second largest lake wholly within the United States.

Below Lake Okeechobee lie the Everglades, one of the few sections of the United States that has never been fully explored. It is inhabited largely by the Seminole Indians, who call it Pa-hay-okee, or "grassy water." The Seminoles retreated to the Everglades after they engaged with the United States in the most costly of its Indian wars.

The Everglades is really a giant tray of water, which acts as a river draining Lake Okeechobee. It is filled with saw grass, clumps of mangrove trees, and islands lush with vegetation. Monotonously flat, the land never rises more than about ten feet above sea level.

Below the Everglades is a string of twenty-five major islands called the Florida Keys, which form an arc, one hundred fifty miles long, southwest of the mainland. While Florida was still controlled by the Spanish, the Keys were inhabited largely by pirates, smugglers, and adventurers. After 1819, when Florida was ceded to the United States, salvaging became the principal trade of the islands, since there were no lighthouses to guide boats through the often dangerous waters. After the 1830s, however, warning systems were installed by the navy, and the islanders turned to cigar making and fishing.

Although the Spanish were exploring and settling Florida long before Europeans entered Georgia, Florida's growth was much slower. Except for the northernmost part of the state, it did not share in pre-Civil War wealth; nor did it share so deeply in the South's defeat. But by the turn of the century, Florida, like Georgia, its neighbor to the north, was becoming a leader of the New South—developing new sources of wealth that would rival in their potential anything the Spanish had dreamed of, or the planters had reaped.

For over a century, Augusta—cotton and textile manufacturing center, situated on the Savannah— has been famous for friendly old-time charm

A few days after our arrival at Augusta, the chiefs and warriors of the Creeks and Cherokees being arrived, the Congress and the business of the treaty came on, and the negociations continued undetermined many days; the merchants of Georgia demanding at least two millions of acres of land from the Indians, as a discharge of their debts, due, and of long standing: the Creeks, on the other hand, being a powerful and proud spirited people, their young warriors were unwilling to submit to so large a demand, and their conduct evidently betrayed a disposition to dispute the ground by force of arms, and they could not at first be brought to listen to reason and amicable terms; however, at length, the cool and deliberate counsels of the ancient venerable chiefs, enforced by liberal presents of suitable goods, were too powerful inducements for them any longer to resist, and finally prevailed. The treaty concluded in unanimity, peace, and good order; and the honourable superintendent, not forgetting his promise to me, at the conclusion, mentioned my business, and recommended me to the protection of the Indian chiefs and warriors. The presents being distributed among the Indians, they departed, returning home to their towns. A company of surveyors were appointed by the governor and council, to ascertain the boundaries of the new purchase; they were to be attended by chiefs of the Indians, selected and delegated by their countrymen, to assist, and be witnesses that the articles of the treaty were fulfilled, as agreed to by both parties in Congress.

WILLIAM BARTRAM
Travels of William Bartram, 1791

Georgia Landscape

A Cotton Boat

The Old Bell Tower

A Model Mill

SCENES AROUND AUGUSTA

*Its wharves and warehouses on a long waterfront,
its dockside activity, its more than a hundred mills
and plants rank it a city of industrial importance*

Soldier's Monument

Cotton Boats Shooting Rapids

C. Graham.

"It was an article of faith in the Confederacy that Northern industry would collapse when cut off from its Southern markets and its supply of cotton. For a while, there was unemployment in cotton mills, but American factory operatives, more mobile and less dependent than their English fellows, returned to the farms whence many of them had come, or shifted into woolen and other industries; and after mid-1862 enough cotton was obtained from occupied parts of the South to reopen many closed mills." The slow normalization that followed during the Reconstruction saw the development of many mills and their communities, as they grew into prosperous manufacturing centers.

SAMUEL ELIOT MORISON

*The Oxford History of
the American People, 1965*

A Characteristic Home.

Georgia's oldest city and busiest seaport, Savannah, typifies the Southern city of grace—stately mansions, cobblestone streets, impeccably kept gardens

Savannah is one of the most attractive cities in the South for a number of reasons, one being the large number of separate, small parks scattered through the downtown area. Besides, one of the greatest trees in America grows well there, and Savannah has taken inspired advantage of it: *Quercus virginiana,* the great live oak. The city is graced with several major park boulevards of four lanes separated by double rows of spreading oaks. The majesty and charm and beauty of these trees defies description. They make Savannah one of the most pleasant places to live in the entire United States. The city is "picturesque," too, and like other seacoast cities, has almost an Old World atmosphere. Much that can be said about New Orleans or Charleston can also be said about Savannah: quiet, "gracious" living, a highly re-fined society of old families, excellent restaurants, a dash of night life. Today, however, Savannah is in commercial turmoil. An old friend, whose insurance offices are located in truly Old World surroundings, expressed the thought that perhaps he should modernize; and when a man of his traditionalism, talks of modernizing, Savannah *is* in turmoil.

CALDER WILLINGHAM
American Panorama, 1947

AUGUSTA, FROM SUMMERVILLE

Along Bull Street and in other sections of the city, many spacious squares are planted with magnificent gardens of magnolias, azaleas, oleanders and evergreens

SAVANNAH, FROM THE RIVER

BULL STREET, SAVANNAH

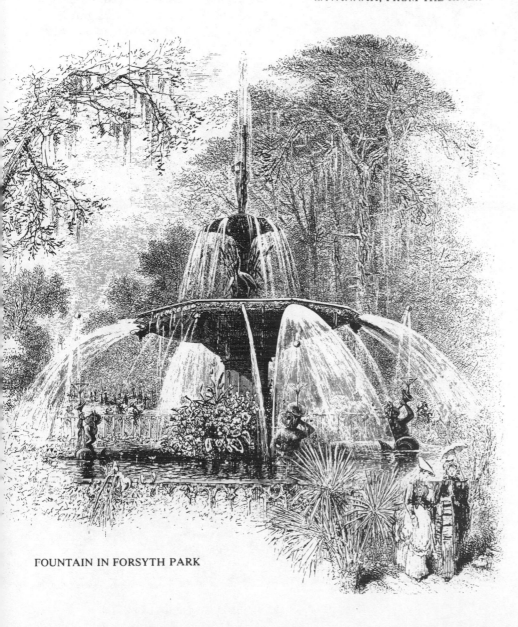

FOUNTAIN IN FORSYTH PARK

Natural beauty is not all that Savannah boasts. Its architecture is varied and striking; much of it in the quaint fashion of by-gone days, but with those characteristics that the art of the present day is eager to counterfeit. It is rich in historic memories; its schools are unsurpassed; its society is cultured; art is patronized, and all the influences exist which make the city attractive.

Every phase of the Southern economy focused on the growing of cotton—every river saw cotton boats and barges— every marketplace teemed with bales by the wagonload

Cotton planting advanced from South Carolina and Georgia across the "black belts" (so called from the color of the soil) and Indian cessions of the Gulf states, occupied the Mississippi valley up to Memphis, pushed up the Red river of Louisiana to Indian Territory, and passed the boundary of Mexico into Texas. On the march King Cotton acquired new subjects: monied immigrants from the North, or ambitious dirt farmers who purchased a slave or two on credit, and with good luck became magnates. In every region fit for cotton, the richest lands were absorbed by plantations during the first generation of settlement. Hunter folk moved westward and poor whites closed in on the gullied hillsides and abandoned fields. Some of the best minds of the South endeavored to arrest this process by scientific methods of agriculture; but as long as good land remained plentiful and cheap, whether within the United States or adjacent under the feeble sovereignty of Mexico, the cotton growers preferred their old ways.

THE SAVANNAH, NEAR AUGUSTA

The tide does not flow above 12 or 14 miles above the City though the River is swelled by it more than double that distance — Rice and Tobacco (the last of wch is greatly increasing) are the principal exports — Lumber & Indigo are also exported but the latter is on the decline, and it is supposed by Hemp & Cotton — Ship timber, viz. live Oak & Cedar is (and may be more so) valuable in the exptn.

PRESIDENT GEORGE WASHINGTON
Diary,
excerpt from May 15, 1791

SPANISH MOSS, BONAVENTURE CEMETERY

*Throughout Georgia, from Albany to Athens, Waco to Waycross
—cotton was king—the ubiquitous mule team hauling crops
over rutty dirt roads for shipment to mill centers*

MARKETPLACE IN A SMALL GEORGIA VILLAGE

Across the Georgia Piedmont, stretching in an undulating plain through the center of the state, is the broad band of regions most vital to the Peach State's economy

FRANKLIN COLLEGE, ATHENS

Rome, in north Georgia, is the capital of the valley-and-hill region, a town built among the hills at the junction of the Oostanaula and Etowah rivers, which form the Coosa. The town is known, among other things, for the nearby Berry Schools and College, a fabulous educational empire created out of nothing, except an iron will and vision, by Miss Martha Berry. The students are chosen almost entirely from the rural South and do not pay to attend; but they all contribute by working (in the field of agriculture, mostly), and thus gain experience along with book learning—an educational system widely admired for many reasons. The campus of the Berry Schools has been called, with justice, the most beautiful in America. It is certainly one of the largest. Miss Martha, by the time of her death, had accumulated more than thirty thousand acres for the "grounds" of her schools.

CALDER WILLINGHAM

American Panorama, 1947

VIEW OF ROME

Here, with the exception of coastal Savannah,
are located the largest cities—Atlanta, Augusta,
Athens, Columbus, La Grange, Macon, Milledgeville

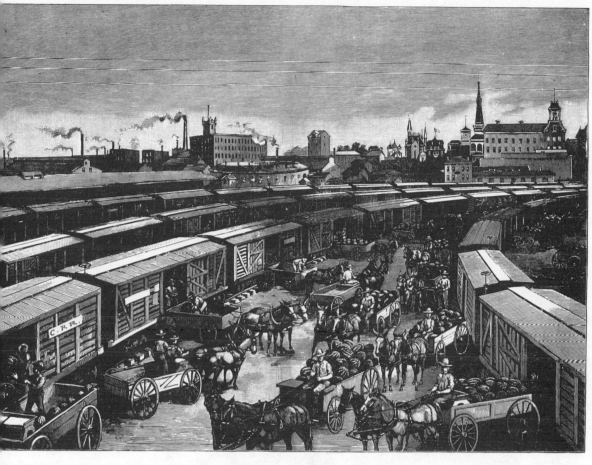

RAILROAD YARDS, ATLANTA

General Sherman's efficient army demolition squads destroyed ninety per cent of Atlanta in 1864, just before he began his historic march to the sea. The city rose from its ashes to become the state's great capital city—the South's largest industrial, financial, and educational center. The visitor in the capital city of the Peach State finds that today it is less the nostalgic city of "Gone with the Wind" than the cultural and economic heart of the Southeast. Peachtree Street is still counted among the South's most famous avenues, but today it is more exciting than it is romantic, for huge new office buildings, apartments, excellent museums, and lavish shops have sprung up along it. Little of Georgia is drowsing beneath the magnolias these days.

Texaco Touring Atlas,
1965

COMMERCIAL CENTRE, ATLANTA

Atlanta—mercilessly battered and burned during the Civil War, when eighty thousand Northern troops destroyed stores, factories, and public buildings . . .

What is the South? It is not what people say it is—and never has been. From the time of the landing of Amadas and Barlowe on Roanoke Island "in Virginia" to the time of Thomas Nelson Page, say from 1584 to 1884, the region was, by its own admission, "the goodliest land under the cope of heaven," peopled by angels in human form, with a few foreign devils from "up North" thrown in by way of contrast. From the time of Page to that of Erskine Caldwell, William Faulkner and Lillian Smith, the South has somehow become transformed into a never-never, Krafft-Ebing land of psychopathia sexualis, peopled by sadists, masochists, rapists, satyrs, nymphomaniacs, and necrophiles, to mention a few of the better known types, together with assorted murderers, arsonists and lynchers, although it seems to draw the line at cannibalism, even during a failure of the turnip crop. The notion that the South is a geographical region of the United States of America, populated by rather easy-going people of various shades of complexion, who live rather ordinary lives . . . is too fantastic a thought to be entertained seriously by writers or readers of modern South literature. . . . The South has become a cross between a Gothic romance and a Greek tragedy rewritten by Freud. . . .

WILLIAM T. POLK
Southern Accent, 1953

On Capitol Avenue.

A Modern Residence

A Peachtree St. Cottage

A Villa

A Doctor's residence.

Cor. Whitehall and Hunter Sts.

On Washington St.

Home of a Merchant

A Suburban Home.

A Peachtree St. residence.

RESIDENCES, ATLANTA

. . . turned immediately, on departure of the enemy, to the task of reconstruction, and within a decade of hectic building activity the "New South" was born

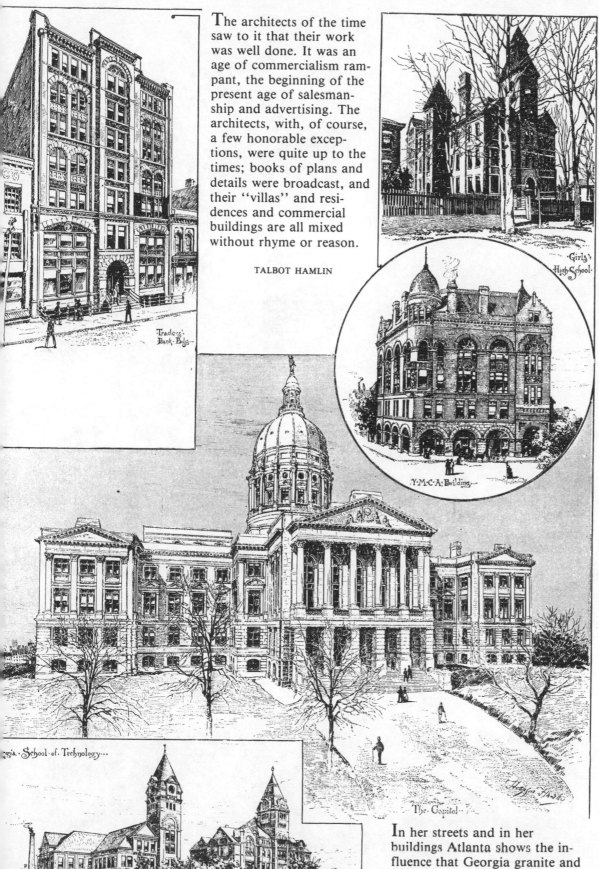

The architects of the time saw to it that their work was well done. It was an age of commercialism rampant, the beginning of the present age of salesmanship and advertising. The architects, with, of course, a few honorable exceptions, were quite up to the times; books of plans and details were broadcast, and their "villas" and residences and commercial buildings are all mixed without rhyme or reason.

TALBOT HAMLIN

The New South is enamored of her new work. Her soul is stirred with the breath of a new life. The light of a grander day is falling fair on her face. She is thrilling with the consciousness of growing power and prosperity. As she stands upright, full-statured and equal among the people of the earth, breathing the keen air and looking out upon the expanding horizon, she understands that her emancipation came because in the inscrutable wisdom of God her honest purpose was crossed and her brave armies beaten.

HENRY W. GRADY
The New South, 1886

In her streets and in her buildings Atlanta shows the influence that Georgia granite and marble has on her architecture. The new State Capitol, in a general way, resembles the Capitol at Washington, and is the work of Edbrook & Burnham, of Chicago.

THE CAPITOL, ATLANTA AND RECENT BUILDINGS

Although Florida was the site of the earliest European settlement
—preceding Jamestown and Plymouth by more than a half-century
—only its northern coastal tip was touched by the Spaniards . . .

Florida is a strange land, both in its traditions and its natural features. It was the first settled of the States, and has the most genial climate of all of them; and yet the greater part of it is still a wilderness. Its early history was one long romance of battle and massacre, and its later annals are almost equally interesting. The Spaniards, who were the first Christian people to visit it, were much impressed with its mystery and its scenery, and, as they discovered it on Easter Sunday, which in their language is called "Pascua Florida," they commemorated the event by giving the new territory its present appellation. The time was when Florida was an immense sand-bar, stretching into the Gulf of Mexico, and probably as barren as can be conceived. But in the semi-tropical climate under which it exists, in the course of ages the seeds carried to its shores by the sea and the winds and the myriads of birds which find it a resting-place, have clothed it with luxuriant vegetation, interspersed with tracts of apparently barren sands. It is a land of peculiar scenery, which the pencil of the artist has heretofore scarcely touched. Its main features illustrate the absurdity of the common notion that the landscapes of tropical and semi-tropical latitudes are superior in luxuriance of vegetable production to those of the temperate zones.

J. B. THORPE

Picturesque America, 1872

LIGHTHOUSE, MOUTH OF ST. JOHN'S RIVER

. . . leaving the wild interior of dense swamps, "grassy water" and crocodile-infested rivers to be penetrated and settled at a much later date

MAKING CYPRESS SHINGLES

In this heat and wetness life breeds and spawns as it has for millions of years. Mostly, it is shy, night-feeding, night-hunting, but you sense its presence and feel that eyes are watching you: the green-glowing eyes of panthers, the liquid eyes of deer, the cold eyes of rattlesnakes and cotton-mouths, the black-masked eyes of raccoons. These last you will probably see as they move across the road with their high-shouldered, flat-footed shuffle, or as with their deft little hands they wash their food in a patch of clear water among the mangroves. A slow swirl in one of the coastal rivers may show where a manatee—fat, wrinkled, childishly blue-eyed—is feeding on water weeds.

BENEDICT THIELEN

GREEN COVE SPRINGS

POST OFFICE ON THE OCKLAWAHA

*Burned and sacked by the English buccaneer Sir Francis Drake,
in 1586—St. Augustine survived slaughter and pillage through
three centuries of occupation by Spanish, French, and English*

The quaint little city of
St. Augustine, Florida, the
oldest European settlement
in the United States, is
situated on the Atlantic
coast, in a narrow penin-
sula formed by the Sebas-
tian and Matanzas Rivers,
on the west side of a harbor which is separated
from the ocean by the low
and narrow island of
Anastasia. It lies about
forty miles south of the
great river St. John's, and
about one hundred and
sixty miles south from
Savannah, in Georgia.

J. B. THORPE

Picturesque America, 1872

ST. MARK'S CASTLE, ST. AUGUSTINE

STREET IN ST. AUGUSTINE

ST. AUGUSTINE CATHEDRAL

Oldest city in the United States, founded in 1565—resort of Tories during the Revolutionary War—rich in Hispanic culture, impregnable forts, fine cathedrals

At St. Augustine as at other points, the Spanish arrivals remained largely soldiers at a far outpost. Twenty years after Menéndez' exploit, Sir Francis Drake made a raid on St. Augustine and burned it to the ground. In 1665 another English freebooter looted it. This time the court ordered a stronger fort, and for decades men worked to erect thirty foot walls, twelve feet across at the base, of coquina or shellstone. Examining the costs, the king said wryly that its bastions must have been made of silver. Still, the Castillo de San Marco was an impressive example of power and grace. Several times the people fled to it, to survive while their community was razed. Today the fort still remains, and so does something of older St. Augustine. The city gates, several times rebuilt, stand where they did when they ordered the early moat, as tall rectangles topped with Moorish designs. A part of St. Augustine lingers as the Southeast's most tangible relic of the Spaniards' bid for power.

HARNETT T. KANE
Gone Are the Days, 1960

WATCHTOWER,
ST. MARK'S CASTLE

THE CITY GATE, ST. AUGUSTINE

INTERIOR, ST. MARK'S CASTLE

CONVENT GATE

Florida's rivers twist and turn through low, trackless sawgrass prairies—the Suwannee, the St. Johns and the Oklawaha—their banks lined with royal palms, gumbo-limbo, mahogany and the strangler fig

But even around the Everglades, intrusions of commerce are causing profound concern for its future as a place for human enjoyment. Yet what survives in this steaming world where life has spawned for millions of years is indeed wondrous. *Pa-hay-okee* in Indian language means "grassy water," which is what the Everglades are: a river of grass. "But their grass is not grass as we know it," writes Benedict Thielen, whose appreciation of the Everglades is that of a lyrical naturalist. "It does not bend and ripple under the wind. It stands stiff, straight, and unyielding. It is really not grass at all but a flowering sedge, one of the oldest forms of green life on earth. It grows with fierce luxuriance, eight, ten, and in some places, fifteen feet high. It is set with tiny, sharp teeth of silica, and this is why they call it saw grass. The blades of this grass are truly blades— they can tear off a man's clothes and rip open his flesh. Like an impenetrable stockade they stand here, upthrust in their countless millions, a wilderness of sharpened swords. Spreading over thirty-five hundred square miles, the saw grass grows in the shallow water, fed by the sun and the deep rich rot of forty centuries of alternating life and death.... The grass does not move. But below it, invisibly, the water moves...from Lake Okeechobee southward, it flows slowly to the sea."

BENEDICT THIELEN

ON THE OCKLAWAHA

The Everglades, in the lower third of the Florida peninsula—covering a vast stretch of grasslands, sloughs and tropical vegetation—sanctuary for the pink ibis, snowy egret, vicious 'gators and wildcats

This is one of the most remote and primitive areas in the United States. Here the resourceful Seminoles finally found sanctuary in the "grass water" prairies out of which rise fertile hammocks, or islands, heavily grown with royal palms, mahogany, tamarind, the redbarked gumbo-limbo, and the cruelly beautiful strangler fig. Here the Indians who refused the indignity of being removed en masse to Oklahoma built their villages and planted their squash and bananas, confident that this insidious marsh country of the redbug and the moccasin would be theirs by default because it was the one section of Florida the white man could not endure. The only other inhabitants of these impenetrable mangrove swamps were squatters, outcasts, moonshiners who lived in shacks raised on stilts over the shallow Florida Bay flats at a now vanished community well-named Snake Bite, or in lawless little bands on the islands of Whitewater Bay.

BUDD SCHULBERG

Florida, in American Panorama, 1947

The Southern Everglades

Shark River.

The Okeechobee

A deserted camp on Okee Chobee.

SCENES IN THE FLORIDA EVERGLADES

*Pensacola, at the extreme northwestern tip of the Sunshine State—
in atmosphere and character more like an old Spanish town—still abides
by the proverb: "The night is made for sleep, and the day for rest"*

The years immediately following the Civil War found Pensacola a drowsy old town, 4 squares wide and 8 long, its streets deep in sand. Upon recovery from the Reconstruction period, Pensacola enjoyed a second era of prosperity, due largely to railroad development of the territory and exports of timber and naval stores. In the early 1870's began the development of the waterfront. The harbor was filled with steamboats and square-riggers from the ports of the world. Vessels, before loading with cargo, discharged their ballast, which was hauled and dumped along the shore, and 60 acres of land were created in a few years. Thus Pensacola's reclaimed shoreline is made up of red granite from Sweden, blue stone from Italy, broken tile from France, and dredgings from the River Themes and the Scheldes of The Netherlands.

FLORIDA

American Guide Series, 1939

SCENES IN PENSACOLA

Down the Ohio... from Pittsburgh to Paducah

ON THE OHIO, BELOW PITTSBURGH

. . . SOUTH PITTSBURGH . . . VIEW OF

THE CITY OF PITTSBURGH . . .

COLUMBUS . . . ASHTABULA . . .

BIG DARBY . . . CINCINNATI . . . PUBLIC

LANDING . . . COURT HOUSE . . . CUSTOM

HOUSE . . . "THE RHINE" . . . NEWPORT

. . . COVINGTON . . . LOUISVILLE . . .

PARKERSBURG . . . JEFFERSONVILLE . . .

NEW ALBANY . . . INDIANAPOLIS . . .

MADISON . . . CAIRO, JUNCTION OF THE

OHIO AND MISSISSIPPI RIVERS

THE OHIO BELOW PITTSBURGH

Down the Ohio... from Pittsburgh to Paducah

I T WAS CALLED "OHIO FEVER"—THE FIRST great push westward after the American Revolution. In 1787 the new congress established the Northwest Territory and opened for settlement the vast region beyond the thirteen original states. By 1811 a manual for river pilots could already tell travelers of the changing face of the newly settled Ohio River valley: "Now the immense forests recede, cultivation smiles along its banks, towns every here and there decorate its shores, and it is not extravagant to suppose, that the

day is not very far distant when its whole margin will form one continued village." The prediction was not extravagant. Today the Ohio River basin is one of the most populated and industrialized regions in the United States.

Settlers flocked west in the thirty years following the opening of the territory. Some came down the Ohio River by flatboat and canoe; others drove Conestoga wagons along the Genesee, Forbe's, Cumberland, and Wilderness roads. By boat or by wagon, they responded to people such as Manasseh Cutler, who told them of "the most agreeable, the most advantageous, the most fertile land which is known to any people of Europe, whatsoever." Some years later, a less enchanted Charles Dickens could observe nothing there but "sky, wood, and water, all the livelong day; and heat that blistered everything it touched." But most settlers, hungry for land and yearning for the freedom of limitless prairies, forest, and mountains, ignored such fastidious objections. In 1811, the *New Orleans* became the first steamboat to sail the Ohio, and by 1837 over three hundred steamboats were churning the river.

At the Ohio's point of origin, where the Allegheny and Monongahela rivers meet, lies Pittsburgh, the first of many cities to flourish as the result of the busy river traffic. Because of its strategic position at the junction of the two rivers, Pittsburgh was an early outpost. Fortified first by the French—who called it Fort Duquesne—and then by the English—who renamed it Fort Pitt—it was already settled as a town in the 1760s. By the end of the eighteenth century, it had become an important shipbuilding center and port of departure for people and goods moving west.

From Pittsburgh, the Ohio flows southwest, through the nation's richest coal country. Wheeling, on the river's eastern bank, is West Virginia's chief river port. East of Wheeling stretch the green hills, ridges, and mountains created millennia ago by great geological upheavals, which also deposited the mineral riches of the region. Upheavals of a more recent nature bitterly rent West Virginia and its people. In 1859 John Brown attempted his abolitionist insurrection at Harpers Ferry, in the easternmost tip of the state. In the years that followed, loyalties to the North and the South split families and friends throughout the state. In the west, miners struggled against the stubborn earth and the equally stubborn mine owners, and along the Kentucky border the Hatfields and McCoys feuded for twenty years.

On the Ohio's western bank lies the state to which the river has given its name. Although it is really the Middle West, Ohio is the place where the Middle West begins, and where, for pioneers heading west, civilization once offered its last outposts. The Cumberland Road— renamed the National Road in the 1830s—

crossed the center of the state; and at Springfield a statue, the *Madonna of the Trail*, stands to commemorate the women who crossed the Ohio to face the harsh frontier. For many, however, the journey would end in this region. Those who did stop founded towns that prospered from fertile land and a century of westward migration.

Columbus, Ohio's capital and second largest city, stands in the center of the state, near the route of the old National Road. South of Columbus lie the Pickaway Plains, where the Shawnees' fierce resistance to European encroachment once bloodied the land. Cincinnati, situated on the river, already had a population of over twenty thousand by the 1830s, and it continued to grow as traffic along the Ohio increased. Although Mrs. Trollope, who established an exotic but unsuccessful "bazaar" there in 1827, found the city's large commerce in hogs distasteful, she recognized that it was 'a city of extraordinary size and importance . . . and every month appears to extend its limits and its wealth."

Southern Illinois is a hilly, wooded land, where the sycamores dominate the forests along the river. North, just above what is today Terre Haute, the Battle of Tippecanoe was fought in 1811 against the great Tecumseh. Farther south, a town of more peaceful memory, New Harmony, was founded in 1814, by George Rapp and his austere society.

On the southern bank of the Ohio, on a low plain where the river breaks over falls, lies Louisville, Kentucky's biggest and economically most important city. A canal was built around the falls in 1830, and the city's fortunes have continued to be largely dependent on the river traffic.

Kentucky, like West Virginia, knew both the bitter divisions of the Civil War and the equally bitter struggles of the miners.

At the very western end of the state the Ohio flows past Paducah, now a prosperous industrial center. Here the river, which in its thousand-mile course has received the waters of the Cumberland, the Wabash, the Kentucky, the Muskingum, and a score of other rivers, is joined by the Tennessee. Then, swollen to its full, it flows into Illinois and ends its own course in a majestic junction with the Mississippi.

*O-He-Yo, the Wyandot word for "fair to look upon"
—la Belle Riviere to the French settlers—became
the Ohio when the name was Anglicized . . .*

Pittsburgh is situated at the conflux of the rivers Monongahela and Alleghany, the uniting of which forms the Ohio. The even soil upon which it is built is not more than forty or fifty acres in extent. It is in the form of an angle, the three sides of which are enclosed either by the bed of the two rivers or by stupendous mountains. The houses are principally brick, they are computed to be about four hundred, most of which are built upon the Monongahela; that side is considered the most commercial part of the town.

F. A. MICHAUX
Travels, 1805

CITY OF PITTSBURGH

These ships were to go, in the spring following, to New Orleans, loaded with the produce of the country, after having made a passage of two thousand two hundred miles before they got into the ocean. There is no doubt but they can, by the same rule, build ships two hundred leagues beyond the mouth of the Missouri, fifty from that of the river Illinois, and even in the Mississippi, two hundred beyond the place whence these rivers flow; that is to say, six hundred and fifty leagues from the sea; as their bed in the appointed space is as deep as that of the Ohio at Pittsburgh; in consequence of which it must be a wrong conjecture to suppose that the immense tract of country watered by these rivers cannot be populous enough to execute such undertakings. The rapid population of the three new western states, under less favourable circumstances, proves this assertion to be true. Those states, where thirty years ago there was scarcely three hundred inhabitants, are now computed to contain upwards of a hundred thousand; and although the plantations on the roads are scarcely four miles distant from each other, it is very rare to find one, even among the most flourishing, where one cannot with confidence ask the owner, whence he has emigrated; or, according to the trivial manner of the Americans, "What part of the world do you come from?"

F. A. MICHAUX
Travels, 1805

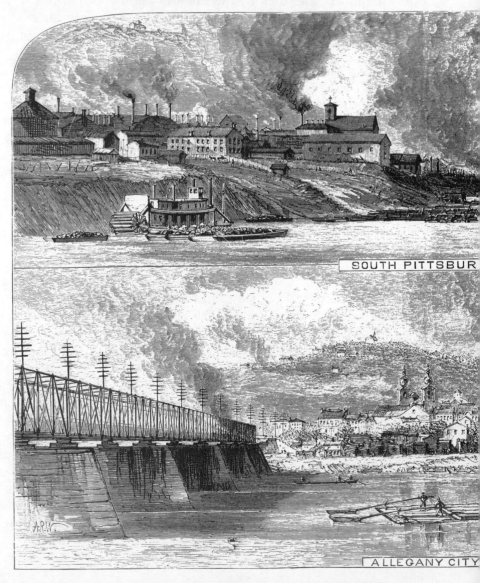

SOUTH PITTSBURGH AND ALLEGHENY CITY

. . . the only major American river flowing westerly—
from the confluence of the Monongahela and the Allegheny
—a strategic junction where Pittsburgh was built

PITTSBURGH, FROM SOLDIERS' MONUMENT

Pittsburgh smoke and fog make strange companions. I remember one murky morning when from the tower of the Allegheny Library the city resolved itself into a steaming caldron, with the sky-scrapers emerging as though a race of giants had been condemned to have their feet parboiled. About this one feature of the local pageant one might run on without end. But any such account as this of the picturesque side of the city of beautiful smoke perforce must rigorously select a mere handful of effects out of as many as would fill fat volumes. On arriving in Pittsburgh the first thought of the wise beauty-lover is to visit Mt. Washington, a height on the further bank of the Monongahela River which offers the best view of the Y shaped city. The Monongahela forms the right prong of the Y, the Allegheny the left. And they flow together into the stem, which is the Ohio. The two prongs are laced with bridges. The apex of the peninsula between them is flat like the toe of a boot. This rises, as the rivers diverge, into a high instep known as "The Hill." So much for geography. The pilgrim crosses the Smithfield Street Bridge, enters the small, misshapen car of one of those startingly European "inclines" that hale him up the crag at an angle of forty-five degrees, or so, and stands straightway upon an eminence. "Above the smoke and stir of this dim spot which men call Pittsburgh."

ROBERT HAVEN SCHAUFFLER
Romantic America, 1913

"Ohio fever"—the great migration to the West—infected thousands who journeyed by Conestoga wagon across the Alleghenies and down the Ohio—the "shining road" . . .

In 1838 Caleb Atwater of Circleville published *A History of Ohio,* the first and most buoyant outline of the state. This Massachusetts Yankee, a failed businessman and lawyer with nine children to support, had soon caught the Ohio excitement. Remarking on Columbus as a seat of government, he stated: Its buildings are, many of them, large, commodious and handsome. The state house is not such a one as Ohio ought to have this day . . . . The penitentiary is a large, handsome building of stone, built mostly by the convicts who are confined in it. . . . That we have prospered [despite hardships and dangers and sufferings] more than any other people did in the world, is most certain; but our exertions to improve our conditions are by no means to be relaxed—to make Ohio what it ought to be, the first state in the Union in numbers, knowledge, wealth, and political power. . . . Our position in the nation is peculiarly felicitous as to soil, climate, and productions, and it will be our own fault if we are not the happiest people in the Union.

CALEB ATWATER
A History of Ohio, 1838

BRIDGE OVER THE BIG DARBY

HOWE TRUSS BRIDGE, ASHTABULA

. . . inspiring the hectic settlement of the Buckeye State
—the spread of rail lines—the spanning of rivers
by bridges of wood, iron, and suspension cable

COVERED RAILROAD BRIDGE, COLUMBUS

I embarked a few years since, at Pittsburg, for Cincinnati, on board of a steam boat—more with a view of realising the possibility of a speedy return against the current, than in obedience to the call of either business or pleasure. It was a voyage of speculation. I was born on the banks of the Ohio, and the only vessels associated with my early recollections were the canoes of the Indians, which brought to Fort Pitt their annual cargoes of skins and bear's oil. The Flat boat of Kentucky, destined only to float with the current, next appeared; and after many years of interval, the Keel boat of the Ohio.

MORGAN NEVILLE
The Western Souvenir, 1829

NEW SUSPENSION BRIDGE OVER THE OHIO, CINCINNATI

Tocqueville, ever the keen observer, described Ohioans as a "people without precedence, without traditions, without habits, without dominating ideas even . . .

Cincinnati, midway along the great artery, gateway to the rich Miami country, took the lead. In 1832 in the *Edinburgh Review* a traveler from Scotland reported: Cincinnati on the Ohio: thirty years ago a forest crossed only by the red man; now a rising town, with 20,000 inhabitants, and increasing at the rate of 1400 houses a year. . . . Our astonishment has been speechless in finding that such a spot possessed in 1815 a Lancastrian school, a public library of 1400 volumes, four printing-offices, and three weekly papers. During Mrs. Trollope's stay, Mr. [Timothy] Flint printed there his 'Western States' in two volumes 8vo; a work that would do honour to a London publisher. She speaks of two museums of natural history, a picture gallery, and an attempt by two artists at an academy of design. After this, what town in England, Scotland, or even Ireland, will turn up its nose at Cincinnati? The men can have little or no leisure. But what must be said of the spirit of the place!

WALTER HAVIGHURST
Ohio, 1976

VIEW OF CINCINNATI, FROM NEWPORT BARRACKS

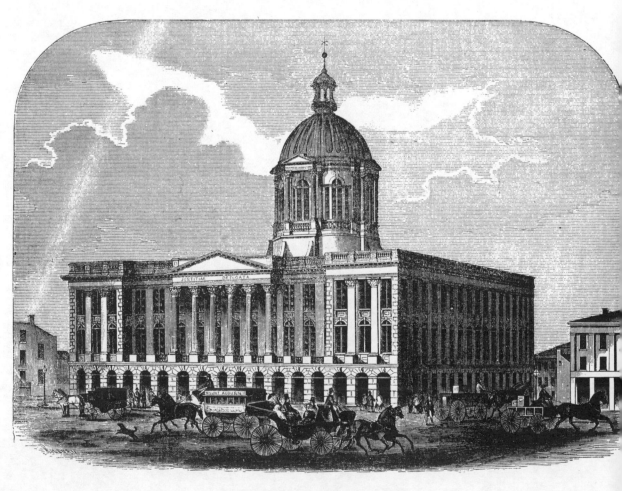

NEW COURT HOUSE, CINCINNATI

. . . cutting out its institutions, like its roads, in the midst of the forests . . . sure to encounter neither limits nor obstacles"

PUBLIC LANDING, CINCINNATI

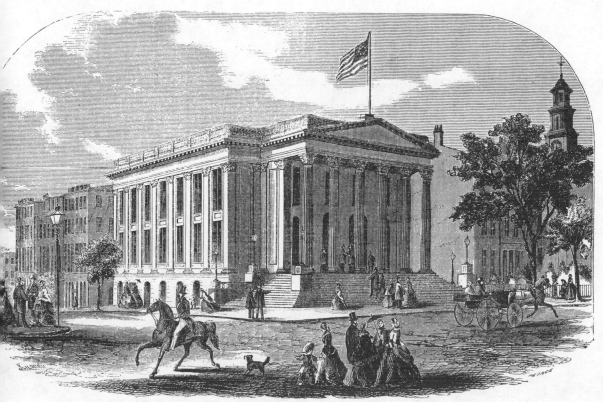

CUSTOM HOUSE AND POST OFFICE, CINCINNATI

MARSHALL DAVIDSON
Life in America, 1951

In the rivalry between the Atlantic ports and New Orleans for the western trade, Cincinnati occupied a strategic place with convenient outlet in either direction, down the Ohio or by way of the Erie Canal. The downriver route was long favored for bulkier products destined for the east coast. At one time eighty per cent of the pork and grain from Cincinnati went down the Ohio. The long line of steamboats and the masses of merchandise piled on the levee were a sign of the "Queen City's" flourishing prosperity. Dickens remarked that it had risen out of the forests like an Arabian Nights city. Even Mrs. Trollope was impressed by the activity along its waterfont. "Its landing is a notable place," she wrote, "extending for more than a quarter of a mile. . . . I have seen fifteen steamboats lying there at once and still half the wharf was unoccupied."

Longfellow called Cincinnati the "Queen City of the West," recognizing its rich cultural heritage —a city founded at the close of the Revolution . . .

During nearly two years that I resided in Cincinnati, or its neighbourhood, I neither saw a beggar, nor a man of sufficient fortune to permit his ceasing his efforts to increase it; thus every bee in the hive is actively employed in search of that honey of Hybla, vulgarly called money; neither art, science, learning, nor pleasure can seduce them from its pursuit. This unity of purpose, backed by the spirit of enterprise, and joined with an acuteness and total absence of probity, where interest is concerned, which might set canny Yorkshire at defiance, may well go far towards obtaining its purpose . . .

"THE RHINE"

CINCINNATI, VIEW FROM THE CARLISLE HOTEL

. . . on the banks of the Ohio—in the southwest corner of the Buckeye State—where Kentuckians, Virginians, and New Englanders welcomed the influx of Germans and Irish, in the forties and fifties

FOURTH STREET, CINCINNATI

. . . Perhaps the most advantageous feature in Cincinnati is its market, which, for excellence, abundance, and cheapness can hardly, I should think, be surpassed in any part of the world, if I except the luxury of fruits, which are very inferior to any I have seen in Europe. There are no butchers, fishmongers, or indeed any shops for eatables, except bakeries, as they are called, in the town; every thing must be purchased at market; and to accomplish this, the busy housewife must be stirring betimes, or, 'spite of the abundant supply, she will find her hopes of breakfast, dinner, and supper for the day defeated, the market being pretty well over by eight o'clock. The beef is excellent, and the highest price when we were there, four cents (about two-pence) the pound. The mutton was inferior, and so was veal to the eye, but it ate well, though not very fat; the price was about the same. The poultry was excellent; fowls or full-sized chickens, ready for the table, twelve cents, but much less if bought alive.

FRANCES TROLLOPE
Domestic Manners of the Americans, 1832

On the Cincinnati riverfront in the spring of 1848 a new bookkeeper began work in a shipping office. His name was Stephen Collins Foster. In his big ledger each page was a packet: *Fairmont, Messenger, Oswego, Bolivar, Ohio Belle, Gladiator, Hibernia.* Outside his window, carts rumbled on the pavement, passengers thronged the wharf boat, and a parade of big white steamers lined the levee. In the chill wind, tatters of smoke blew from the tall chimneys. But the river led to the languid, fragrant Southland. Stephen Foster had melodies in his mind. Forgetting bills of lading, he began to write:

> I come from Alabama
> Wid my banjo on my knee.
> I'm gwan to Louisiana
> My true love for to see.
> Oh! Susanna, do not cry for me.
> I come from Alabama,
> Wid my banjo on my knee.

WALTER HAVIGHURST
Ohio, 1975

"THE RHINE"

Across the Ohio, from Cincinnati, are Newport and Covington —satellite towns in neighboring Kentucky, the Bluegrass State, famous for its breeding of horses and the Derby

Steamboat travel was both glamorous and squalid. The stately four-deckers, white as a wedding cake, had floral carpets, inlaid woodwork, and oil paintings on the stateroom doors. They provided a nursery, a barbershop, gaming rooms, and a gleaming bar. Their cabin passengers sat down to five-course dinners with orchestra music. But most of the travelers never saw the splendors of the grand saloon. Immigrants, woodsmen, and frontier farmers were crowded among cargo and livestock on the lower deck, cooking porridge on the boiler flues and drinking river water. They slept on bales and boxes. Living close to the engines and the waterline, they were the first victims of collision and explosion. The one inducement to deck passage was economy. For a dollar a decker could travel five hundred miles—one-fifth the fare for cabin passengers.

WALTER HAVIGHURST
Ohio, 1975

MARKET AND SQUARE, COVINGTON, KENTUCKY

NEWPORT BARRACKS ON THE OHIO

On the falls of the Ohio—downriver about 130 miles from Cincinnati—lies Louisville, where many an early traveler broke his journey and settled down

SPEED MARKET, LOUISVILLE

Because Lexington is known as the center of Thoroughbred breeding, many of the uninitiated think the Kentucky Derby is run there. It isn't. It's run at Louisville's Churchill Downs. Louisville is Kentucky's biggest city and, businesswise at least, its most important. Its residents estimate a metropolitan district that counts more than half a million. It lies on a low plain where the Ohio River broke over falls as lucrative to early-day pilots, porters and towline hands as they were vexing to vessels and crews. The falls aren't impressive any more. The Government system of locks and dams has reduced them substantially. Until about 1870 the city's prosperity rose and fell with river traffic, in which the steamboat made its first entrance in 1811. A good many northerners terminated their river journeys at Louisville— which accounts for the fact that the town still casts a lusty if not majority Republican vote. "Louisville," says the Kentucky WPA guidebook of 1939, "is a border metropolis that blends the commerce and industry of a Northern city with the Southern city's enjoyment of living." It might have said that Louisville is a big, friendly, country town, notable by outward reputation as the home of the *Courier-Journal*, the Louisville Slugger and the Derby.

A. B. GUTHRIE, JR.
Kentucky, 1947

GREEN AND SIXTH STREETS, LOUISVILLE

*River traffic comprised every type of craft—
from simple raft or flat-bottomed keelboat,
called "broadhorn"—steered by long oars . . .*

To Pittsburgh in the early years came families worn and weary from a punishing journey across the mountains. Some had jolted over the rocky road in cart or wagon. Some had left the wagon broken at a fording place and come on, trundling a few goods in a wheelbarrow. Many had measured, step by step, the Allegheny ridges; years, later a Marietta woman remembered her mother leading a reluctant cow, leaning on the creature during the long way up and over Laurel Mountain. For all, it was the dream of a river flowing west that kept them going. At Pittsburgh, at last, they saw the Monongahela and the Allegheny join to form the dreamed Ohio. After the looming barrier ridges, after the dark trace hemmed in forest, after mud and mire, rocks, roots, and tree stumps, there lay the river, the beckoning, sunlit river winding westward between the wild green shores. This was the main channel of the westward rush, the current that carried the greatest tide of settlement and expansion the world has known. All their lives the immigrants would remember that shining road, like a gift, like a promise, like God's providence in an unfeeling world . . .

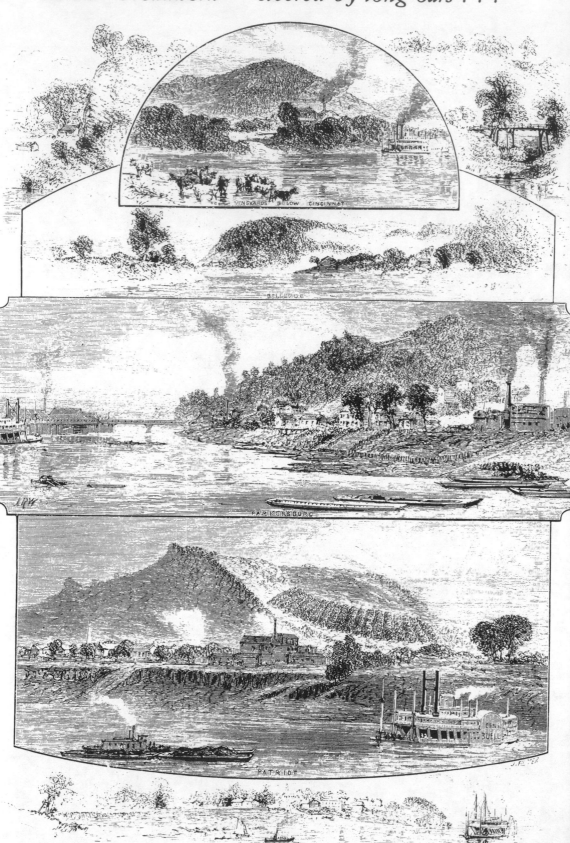

SCENES ON THE OHIO

. . . to the ornate, romantic, stern-wheeled packets—the "river queens"—carrying hundreds of passengers on triple decks, with all the amenities of an exclusive hotel

RAILROAD BRIDGE, PARKERSBURG, WEST VA.

At the Pittsburgh boatyards thirty-five dollars would buy an oblong flat-bottomed craft with a shedlike shelter for its people and a railed deck for horses and cattle. Commonly called a "broadhorn," it had a pair of long steering oars set in timber crotches on the shed roof. Like a floating barnyard it moved down the shining road, horses munching at a pile of hay and chickens scratching at their feet. On the roof a woman rocked a cradle and a man leaned on the steering oar while the tireless river carried them toward the future. By a great gift of geography the promised land of Ohio had a moving, gleaming highway to bring its people home. At Wheeling a flatboat family could put in for stores— salt pork, hominy, dried apples, cornmeal, and molasses. Then on the way again, past great headlands, little creek mouths, long, curved willow islands, and shelves of green bottomland under the lifting hills. While the changing shores slid past, emigrant families talked of lands they would claim, houses they would build, harvests they would gather. The flatboat was a one-way craft. At journey's end it was broken up and put together again as a one room dwelling.

WALTER HAVIGHURST

Ohio, 1975

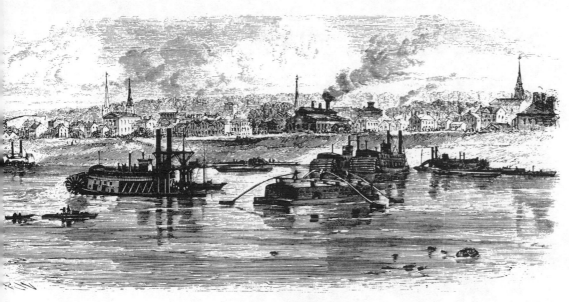

NEW ALBANY, INDIANA

JEFFERSONVILLE, INDIANA

Indianapolis, centered in the Hoosier State, the largest state capital after Boston—chosen in 1821 in newly acquired Indian Territory . . .

In 1818 at St. Mary's, Ohio, three Indiana commissioners met a group of Indian chiefs and bought from them the entire central section of Indiana. Surveyors soon divided this "New Purchase" into townships, and settlement began. In this district a site was chosen for the new Hoosier capital; the town was laid out by a young English engineer, Elias Pym Fordham, who had come to America with Morris Birkbeck. In 1824 four farm wagons moved the seat of government from the old State House at Corydon to the new, centrally located capital.

WALTER HAVIGHURST

Land of the Long Horizons, 1960

VIEW OF MADISON, INDIANA

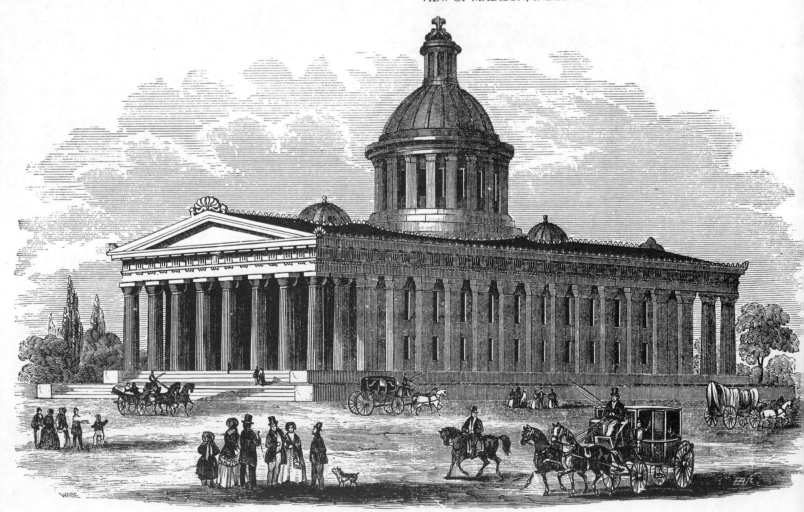

STATE HOUSE, INDIANAPOLIS

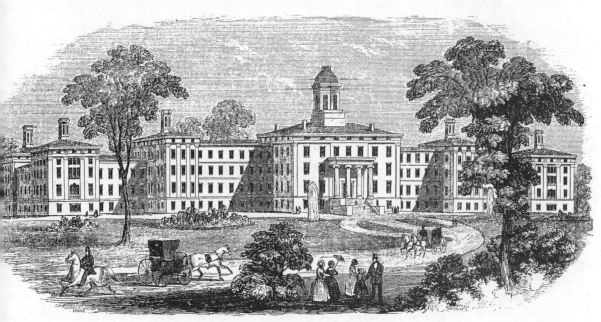

. . . built sturdily in classical style—the seat of government and its institutions expressing a solidity unmatched in other young Midwest communities

STATE HOSPITAL, INDIANAPOLIS

The principal reason for transferring the seat of government from Corydon to Indianapolis was that Corydon was inaccessible to settlers moving into the north and central areas of the state. In 1825 only two stage lines led to the town, one from Centerville and one from Madison. The only other main routes in the state were the Vincennes-New Albany trail, and another from New Albany by way of Salem, Bedford, and Bloomington to Lafayette. Neither of these directly served the new capital.

WILLIAM E. WILSON

Indiana, 1966

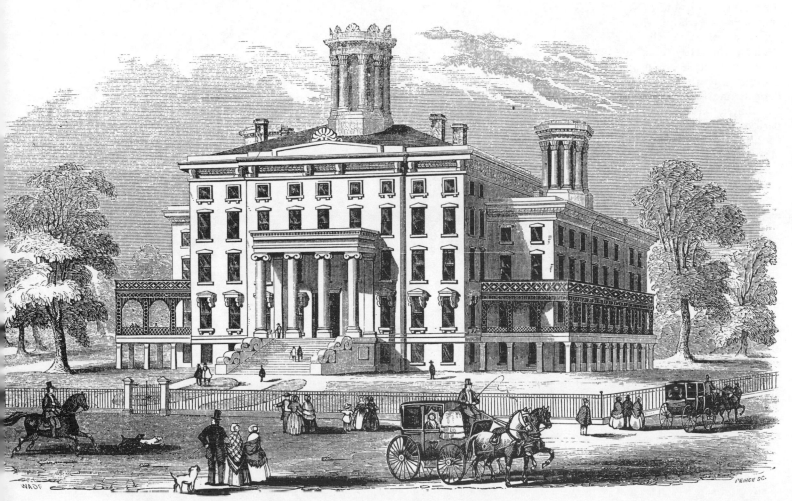

INSTITUTE FOR THE BLIND, INDIANAPOLIS

Downstream, the Ohio flows past Paducah and reaches Cairo, where it meets the Mississippi—forming the junction of three states: Illinois, Kentucky, and Missouri

On they toiled through great solitudes, where the trees upon the banks grew thick and close; and floated in the stream; and held up shrivelled arms from out the river's depths; and slid down from the margin of the land, half growing, half decaying, in the miry water. On through the weary day and melancholy night: beneath the burning sun, and in the mist and vapour of the evening: on, until return appeared impossible, and restoration to their home a miserable dream. They had now but few people on board, and these were as flat, as dull, and stagnant, as the vegetation that oppressed their eyes. No sound of cheerfulness or hope was heard; no pleasant talk beguiled the tardy time; no little group made common cause against the dull depression of the scene. But that, at certain periods, they swallowed food together from a common trough, it must have been old Charon's boat, conveying melancholy shades to judgment. At length they drew near New Thermopolae; where, that same evening, Mrs. Hominy would disembark. A gleam of comfort sunk into Martin's bosom when she told him this. Mark needed none; but he was not displeased. It was almost night when they came alongside the landing-place. A steep bank with an hotel, like a barn, on the top of it; a wooden store or two, and a few scattered sheds.

CHARLES DICKENS

Martin Chuzzlewit, 1844

CAIRO, AT THE JUNCTION OF OHIO AND MISSISSIPPI RIVERS

CANAL LOCKS, MUSKINGUM, OHIO

West of the Appalachians...
& South to the Gulf

THE TENNESSEE RIVER . . .

CUMBERLAND GAP . . . EAGLE CLIFF

. . . KNOXVILLE . . . CHATTANOOGA . . .

LOOKOUT MOUNTAIN . . . FERRY AT

CHATTANOOGA . . . MOBILE BAY . . .

GRANT'S PASS . . . FORT MORGAN . . .

CITY HALL AND NEW MARKET . . .

MONTGOMERY . . . THE CAPITOL . . .

ALABAMA RIVER . . . LOADING COTTON

. . . PLANTER'S HOME . . . FLOODS IN

ALABAMA

THE TENNESSEE

West of the Appalachians...
& South to the Gulf

AT THE TIME OF THE AMERICAN REVO-
lution, the land west of the Appalachian Mountains was still largely unexplored. Cities and towns
lined the Atlantic coast and settlers had pushed
inland. But the rugged mountain range that
cuts across the United States from Canada
almost to the Gulf of Mexico stopped all but
the most intrepid explorers. By the last decades

of the eighteenth century, however, buckskin-
clad frontiersmen were crossing the mountains,
scouting trails and hearing the Indians' tales of
the land farther to the west. Soon the "long
hunters" in the lowlands of Virginia and the
Carolinas were making regular forays into the
mountains, stalking elk, buffalo, deer, and
bear; they often spent months in the uncharted
wilderness. These hunters brought back reports

that excited the imaginations of men who were already growing tired of the "crowded" East.

The most famous of these men, Daniel Boone, crossed the mountains in 1769 and "saw with pleasure the beautiful level of Kentucky." He described it as a second paradise. Later, he moved his family and a large party of settlers through the Cumberland Gap and into central Kentucky. As they made their way across the Appalachians they carved the Wilderness Road, and thereby opened the West to settlement. Following men like Daniel Boone, thousands of settlers were soon traveling the Wilderness Road or taking the longer journey by river. By the turn of the century, settlement had reached such proportions that both Kentucky and Tennessee were admitted to the Union.

To men first seeing these new lands, they must indeed have seemed a second paradise. Where the Cumberland and Pine mountains begin to slope down into eastern Kentucky, they form steep valleys and sharp ridges, canyons and natural rock arches. Laurel azalea and tulip trees bloom on the slopes, and beyond the hills stretch the bluegrass plains.

After selling some Kentucky land to white settlers, a Cherokee Chief, Dragging Canoe, warned that although the land was indeed beautiful, it was "under a cloud and a dark and bloody ground." His warning proved true. In frontier days, settlers were prey both to Indian attacks and to the lawlessness that reigned in those loosely organized lands. In the middle of the nineteenth century bitter divisions over secession pulled families and friends apart, and some of the bloodiest battles of the war itself were fought in Tennessee: Shiloh, Chattanooga, and Knoxville. After the war the Ku Klux Klan was born in Tennessee, and, in more recent times, Harlan County, Kentucky became the scene of bloody industrial strife.

Although Kentucky and Tennessee have given the nation some of its most violent moments, they have also provided some of its most pleasurable ones. Kentucky's bluegrass country is famed both for the music to which it has given its name, and for one of the finest breeds of race horse, the thoroughbred. In Louisville the Derby has been run on the first Saturday of every May, since 1875. The blues were born on Memphis's Beale Street, and in Nashville, the "Athens of the South," country music has coexisted with some of the South's oldest academies.

Alabama had its earliest European settlement as early as 1710, when Sieur de Bienville established Mobile as the capital of French Louisiana. Although Mobile itself remained a fairly busy port, settlers came to Alabama in large numbers only after the end of the eighteenth century. Except for the mountainous northeast, where the Cumberland plateau ends, Alabama is a rolling plain, once inhabited by the Creek, Cherokee, Choctaw, and Chicksaw Indians. Defeated by Andrew Jackson at Horseshoe Bend in 1814, they retreated west and left the state free for European settlement.

Farmers moved south from Tennessee, west from Georgia, and north through the port of Mobile. They were all seeking more land on which to raise the cotton that was enriching the South. They found it in Alabama's rich black belt, so named for the color of its fertile soil. Farms were first established in the center of the state, in the area drained by the Alabama and Tombigbee rivers; but by 1850 most of Alabama was covered both by the fabled great plantations of the Old South and by countless smaller farms.

Most of Alabama's early wealth was agricultural, largely derived from cotton. After the Civil War, when the cotton market crashed, most of Alabama's wealth disappeared. Railroads were built there only during Reconstruction, when coal mining also began. Birmingham was founded in 1870 and quickly became the South's leading iron and steel producer; its roaring blast furnaces form a striking contrast to the largely rural character of the state.

Mobile was the haven for Confederate ships running the Union blockade, and it was the scene of the Civil War's greatest naval battle, finally won by the Union's Admiral D. G. Farragut. Mobile is still a city of stately pre-Civil War homes and lush, carefully tended gardens. Montgomery, in the center of the state, at the head of Alabama River navigation, became the state's capital in 1847, and the capital of the Confederacy in 1861. Jefferson Davis was inaugurated as President of the Confederacy on the steps of the capitol building.

Intrepid frontiersman Daniel Boone blazed the Wilderness Road through Cumberland Gap—a natural pass in the mountains where Virginia, Kentucky, and Tennessee meet

The approach to the range from the northeast side, after leaving Abingdon, Virginia, is over a rough, broken country; and the only compensation to the traveller, as he saunters along on horseback, is in the enjoyment of bits of scenery wherein rocks and running streams, mountain-ferries, quaint old-fashioned mills, farm-houses and cabins perched like birds among the clefts of hills, lovely perspectives, wild-flowers and waving grain, and a homely but hospitable people, combine in charming confusion to keep the attention ever on the alert. The road through the gap, winding like a huge ribbon, to take advantage of every foot of rugged soil, up, down, and around the mountains, is but the enlarged war-trail of the ancient Cherokees and other tribes, who made incursions from one State to the other. You are following the path pursued by Boone and the early settlers of the West. Passing through the scenes of bloody ambuscades, legends, and traditions, it would seem almost a part of the romance of the place if now an Indian should suddenly break the reigning silence with a war-whoop, and its dying echoes be answered by the rifle-shot of a pioneer. In short, it is an old, old region, covered with the rime of centuries, and but slightly changed by the progress of events.

F. G. DE FONTAINE

Picturesque America, 1872

CUMBERLAND GAP, FROM EAGLE CLIFF

Thousands of settlers followed Boone's trail—an endless chain of hopeful pioneers blazing a path of empire, either by wagon or trudging along by shank's mare

CUMBERLAND GAP, FROM THE EAST

The "ridges" referred to are among the curiosities of the Cumberland region. Aside from the fact that they observe a species of parallelism to each other, they contain numerous "breaks," or depressions, which, in the peculiar configuration of the country, appear to the traveller who is at the foot of the mountain to be distant only a few hundred rods; yet he must frequently ride for miles through a labyrinth of hills, blind roads, and winding paths, before he can reach the entrance and pursue his journey. The chief and most celebrated of these great fissures, or hall-ways, through the range, is known as "Cumberland Gap." This gap is situated in East Tennessee, near the Kentucky border, about one hundred and fifty miles southeast from Lexington, and may be regarded as the only practical opening, for a distance of eighty miles, that deserves the name of a "gap." There are other places which are so called, but it is only for the reason that they are more easy of access than because of any actual depression in the mountain. At a place called "Rogers's Gap," for example, which is eighteen miles distant from Cumberland Gap, there is no gap whatever; but the road, taking advantage of a series of ridges on the northern side, and running diagonally on the southern side, is rendered, with great exertion, passable by man and beast.

F. G. DE FONTAINE
Picturesque America, 1872

Originally known as the state of Franklin—Tennessee has three regions that differ vastly from one another: scenic mountains in the east, with Knoxville its leading city . . .

In 1786, twenty-five years after the first white man traveled through the region, Captain James White built a log cabin near the present Farragut Hotel, and became Knoxville's first settler. During the Civil War, because the majority of East Tennesseans were loyal to the union, a Confederate army of occupation was sent into the area in 1861; two years later, in preparation for battles around Chattanooga these troops were withdrawn, to be followed by a Federal force under the command of Major General A. E. Burnside. Confederate troops under Longstreet tried to capture the city by direct assault, and after heavy losses by both sides his army retired to winter quarters near Morristown. When peace came, the city's restoration was rapid. Industries that have sprung up, mainly in cotton textiles, marble, and hardwood furniture. Knoxville is the uppermost terminal of the navigable portion of the Tennessee River.

The American Guide, 1949

Lyon's View.

An Old-Time Hut.

Private Residence.

KNOXVILLE AND VICINITY

. . . the vast Bluegrass area in the center, with Nashville its classic capital; and, on the banks of the Mississippi, Memphis—"heartbeat of the West"

Knoxville University

OXVILLE from across the River.

Marble Barges.

Nevertheless, certain differences persist. Nashville, the second largest city and capital of the state and of Middle Tennessee, has a serene, Athenian quality, as if it were more attuned to its eight universities and colleges than to its industrial plants. A Nashvillian speaks more readily of his city's book houses and writers, its symphony and its statelier past, than of its more material promise. Memphis lacks this quiet assurance, for it grew from a brawling boom town on the river to the state's largest city so hurriedly that it has hardly had time to assess itself. Energetic, clean and preoccupied with its almost incredible industrial expansion. Memphis seems—despite its Beale Street, its heavy Negro population, its Cotton Carnival, and a commanding position as the deep South's cotton-trade center—more like a bustling Midwestern city than the mecca of Mississippi planters.

HODDING CARTER
American Panorama, 1947

Lookout Mountain, on the fringe of the city of Chattanooga, is famed as both a scenic and historic site, where Civil War legions fought the dramatic "Battle of the Clouds" . . .

East Tennessee, Middle Tennessee, West Tennessee. So much in each of which a man might boast. The refashioned river itself; Fall Creek Falls, with a water drop of 265 feet, the highest east of the Rockies. And Lookout Mountain dominating Moccasin Bend, a lofty rock-faced promontory carved through thousands of years by the downrushing Tennessee. From Lookout Mountain, a man can see seven states on a clear day. If he is a good Tennessean, he will prefer the nearest. And within the state, he will prefer his section and the city which dominates it. Time was when the four principal cities of Tennessee could be defined by characteristics as well as by location. This is less true now, for a common industrialization tends to level their differences. They share a determination to grow, to industrialize.

HODDING CARTER

American Panorama, 1947

CHATTANOOGA AND THE TENNESSEE, FROM LOOKOUT MOUNTAIN

. . . on the summit and in the nearby regions of Missionary Ridge and Chickamauga—where huge armies of the North and South maneuvered, battled, and retrenched

LOOKOUT MOUNTAIN, FROM THE "POINT"

On the summit of Lookout Mountain the northwest corner of Georgia and the northeast extremity of Alabama meet on the southern boundary of Tennessee. The mountain lifts abruptly from the valley to a height of fifteen hundred feet. It is the summit overhanging the plain of Chattanooga that is usually connected in the popular imagination with the title of Lookout, but the mountain really extends for fifty miles in a southwesterly direction into Alabama. The surface of the mountain is well wooded, it has numerous springs, and is susceptible of cultivation. In time, no doubt, extensive farms will occupy the space now filled by the wilderness. There is a small settlement on the crest of the mountain, consisting of two summer hotels, several cottages and cabins, and a college. It is a grand place for study, and the young people of this sky-aspiring academy have certainly superb stimulants in the exhilarating air and glorious scenes of their mountain *alma mater.*

O. B. BUNCE
Picturesque America, 1872

Rising amid lakes and lofty peaks of the Cumberlands, to the east—the great Tennessee River twists its tortuous course, turning first south into Alabama, and then north

Under the intelligent direction of Lieut. Adams of the United States Army, the Government is now endeavoring to remove the obstructions and widen the channel, which at this point is narrowed from the average of six hundred feet to two hundred and fifty; and hence the novel and picturesque sight of a steamer struggling up against an adverse current by means of a windlass on the bank, with the songs and shouts of the laboring deck-hands, will soon be, if it is not now, a thing of the past. To visit this famous "Suck," and get a sketch or two of the shore, was the purpose of our journey along the Tennessee. The three days of wintry airs on Lookout Mountain had made out-of-door sketching chilling work, but now a soft and balmy April day invited us upon the jaunt; so Mr. Fenn packed his sketching-traps; a vehicle stout in spring, and equal to the vicissitudes of a rough and rocky road, was procured, and we sallied forth.

O. B. BUNCE
Picturesque America, 1872

STEAMER ON THE TENNESSEE, WARPED THROUGH THE "SUCK"

THE TENNESSEE AT CHATTANOOGA

A small town before the Civil War, Chattanooga, on the banks near the Georgia border, became an important military center after its capture by the Federalists

FERRY POINT AT CHATTANOOGA

The method adopted at this ferry is occasionally found in the South, but, ordinarily, ferry-boats are carried from one side of the stream to the other by means of a suspended rope from shore to shore. The Chattanooga ferry is very picturesque, apart from the method of progression. In busy times a sort of tender accompanies the larger boat, and upon this our carriage, with some difficulty, was driven. Boat and tender were crude in construction, old, and dilapidated. The main vessel had a small enclosure, of a hen-coop suggestiveness, which was called a cabin, and which, at a pinch, might give shelter to three or four people. The groups upon its decks were striking. There were sportsmen with their Texan saddles and wide *sombreros*, vehicles, and groups of cattle, all mingled with the most happy contrast of color and form. On the opposite shore, as we drew near, were visible great numbers of waiting horsemen and cattle, giving evidence of the active business of the ferry, and emphasizing the wonder that the bridge has not been restored.

O.B. BUNCE
*Picturesque
America, 1872*

A KENTUCKY ROAD, FROM CUMBERLAND GAP

In Montgomery—Alabama's capital, and first capital of the Confederacy—hundreds of thousands of cotton bales were shipped each year, though now superseded by cattle and hogs

THE CAPITOL, MONTGOMERY

Northern Alabama when I first knew it was a mountain country with a river running through it. Hill cabins perched dangerously on steep acres high above the Tennessee ("Fire your shotgun up the chimley and your punkin crop'll drop into the fireplace"). It was a land of fiddlers' conventions and all-day sings and square dances and court weeks. Few Negroes lived here—their homes were in the Black Belt towns where their slave ancestors had worked for rich white folks. The mountain people plowed their acres six days a week and on the seventh attended little unpainted churches where the wrath of a jealous God was expounded with emphasis. Now this area, because of the damming of the Tennessee River, is a lake country. The rutted roads that once ran near the river are gone, and blacktops run smooth along the ridges from which motorists look down on families picnicking beside clear water.

CARL CARMER

American Panorama, 1947

WATCH AND BELL TOWER, MOBILE

Reminiscent of its past: its Spanish and French heritage,
Mobile—at the head of Mobile Bay, on the Gulf of Mexico—
is an important seaport serving diversified interests

CITY HALL AND NEW MARKET, MOBILE

LIGHTHOUSE, CHOCTAW POINT, MOBILE

GRANT'S PASS, NEAR MOBILE

Mobile stays in the heart, loveliest of cities. I have made many journeys down the Black Warrior and I have always found happiness at its mouth. And so I summarize my impressions rather than tell the story of a visit. Few travelers "pass through" Mobile. The old city rests apart, remembering the five flags that have flown over her. Spain and France and England and the Old South, grown harmonious through the mellowing of time, are echoes in the streets. But since only people who "are going to Mobile" are her visitors, her charms have been less exploited than those of any of the other sea cities of the South. Whether you come by train or by boat, you arrive in the same part of town. There is a smell of hemp and tar about it. Long low two-story buildings, their intricate iron balconies interrupted here and there by signs—"Sailors' Supplies," "The Army and Navy Store," line the narrow streets. Sometimes the balcony overhangs the sidewalk and makes a roofed passage for pedestrians, ornate iron pillars supporting it at the street's edge. These buildings once housed a roistering assembly. The crews of ocean windjammers found liquor here in gilded saloons. They lined up at the mirrored bar with the bully-boys of North Alabama—keel-boatmen on the Black Warrior, planters' sons arrived by side-wheel steam packet from the wide estates on the Tombigbee, badman gamblers in extravagant apparel. The waterfront itself is no longer as picturesque as it was in the days of the clipper ships or the river packets. The gay welter of colorful types has disappeared.

CARL CARMER
Stars Fell on Alabama, 1934

Once an Indian settlement, Mobile became a French colonial capital when Jean Baptiste Le Moyne came ashore in 1702, followed by the British in 1763—an occupation of short duration . . .

The air is soft in Mobile—filled with sea moisture. The tropics reach toward the town from the south. Palms raise straight trunks to the greening tufts that cap them. Fig trees and oleanders, magnolias and Cape Jasmine, Cherokee roses and azaleas make the breezes heavy with sweet odor through the long warm season. It is a gentle air. Like the atmosphere that the people of Mobile create among themselves, it is friendly and easy-going. It folds with equal warmth about the white pillars lifted by a retired Black Belt planter and the wrought-iron patterns of a façade conceived by a French immigrant. Unlike the New Orleans Creoles, with their enclosed patios, Mobile's Latin colonists chose to build homes that looked out on the world. The lawns on which the French and Spanish houses rest have been green for almost two centuries. Outside the commercial streets down by the waterfront, Mobile is a city of leisured space. The old part of the town is a honeycomb of exquisite design. Fleurs-de-lis in formal grace adorn a balcony that faces a wild profusion of grape clusters across the street. The bees of Napoleon, were they to take flight from their iron frame, might light upon the roses of Provence that clamber over the railing of both upper and lower galleries next door. At the city market, once the Spanish government buildings, the iron curves have a cleaner, freer sweep and they turn more delicately against the white stone.

OUR FLEE

VIEW OF

Grant's Pass.

SCENES AROUND MOBILE

. . . for in 1780 the Spanish superseded the British. An American force under General James Wilkinson seized the city in 1813—site of the famous Battle of Mobile Bay

MOBILE.

MOBILE ALA.

Fort Morgan.

Mobile has not always been a city on a byway. In the days of her glory the big-hatted, bright-waistcoated planter brought his wife and daughters down the Black Warrior for the theater, the horse racing, the shopping. Perhaps they embarked at Wetumpka on the famous *St. Nicholas*, its calliope tooting out *Life on the Ocean Wave* to the panic of negroes along the shore. Or they may have come from Gainesville down the Tombigbee on that gorgeous packet *Eliza Battle*, fated to be consumed in flame with a loss of forty lives. In a bayou up the Warrior, a few miles from Mobile, lie many of the sisters of these ships. In that graveyard of the steamboats few names are discernible now. Perhaps the *Southern Belle* rests there, and the *Orline St. John*, the *Ben Lee*, stern-wheeler, the *Allen Glover* (named for her planter owner) . . . . Though these days are memories now, the city has not forgotten. With all its outward semblance of calm, Mobile is gayest of American cities. Its free spirit, less commercialized than that of New Orleans, has kept its Gallic love of the fantastic and amusing. Behind the ornate balconies and long French windows that sedately face the streets, live a people to whom carnival is a natural heritage.

CARL CARMER
Stars Fell on Alabama, 1934

Picking, harvesting, and baling the cotton crop—for shipment to market—presented the planter with problems for which he managed to find various and often ingenious solutions

LOADING COTTON ON THE ALABAMA RIVER

Only a small percentage of the Southern whites had owned slaves, but cotton had opened new visions of riches. Since the beginning of the century there had been much to turn our heads from the older and slower ways of building up a property. The breathless speed at which certain manufacturers had grown, the easy money to be made in starting banks, the speculation in Western lands, the risks of commerce in the war, the rapid rise in city real estate as population concentrated, and the effect of the cotton gin, had all been breeding a spirit which demanded riches overnight instead of by efforts of a lifetime of toil. In the South everyone turned to cotton. "The lawyer, and the doctor, and the schoolmaster, as soon as they earned any money, bought land and negroes, and became planters . . .

PLANTER'S HOME IN ALABAMA

Throughout the South, many rivers became broad highways of commerce, offering a changing spectacle that touched not only the life of travelers, but that of the people on shore

COTTON CHUTE

LOADING COTTON

. . . The preacher who married a rich heiress or rich widow, became owner of a plantation. The merchant who wished to retire from the perplexities of business . . . passed his old age in watching the cotton plant spring up from the fresh-plowed ground." But as the slave trade had been prohibited, the price of slaves advanced rapidly. It was estimated in 1839 that a planter could get a thousand acres of good cleared cotton land for $10,000.

JAMES TRUSLOW ADAMS
The Epic of America, 1933

The rivers of Alabama served to speed the flow of goods—but they were also frequently the cause of much havoc and destruction by flooding of their low-lying banks

Fortunately, a flooding river sometimes overflows its banks or bursts its levees slowly enough to allow evacuation of endangered populations. But not always. Sometimes, a flood wave, or waves, can make a river, or convergence of rivers, crest so much more quickly and higher than expected that the results are as sudden and as deadly as those produced by the burst dam or flash flood. More often, the river flood kills by inches, destroying all a community has worked for in the past, and sometimes all possibility of future subsistence. In terms of regularity and damage, river floods are the worst enemy, though much has been done to effect their control. Dams and reservoirs have been built to control river flooding, as well as levees that are most effective. There are places where a river will flood, no matter what.

WOODY GELMAN and
BARBARA JACKSON

Disaster Illustrated, 1976

FLOODS IN ALABAMA

Down the Mississippi...
from St. Louis to the Gulf

GRAND TOWER ROCK . . . LEVEE AT

ST. LOUIS . . . LOCUST STREET . . .

VERANDA ROW . . . COURT HOUSE . . .

MERCANTILE LIBRARY . . . ST. CHARLES

RAILROAD BRIDGE . . . STREET SCENES

IN ST. LOUIS . . . VICKSBURG . . .

MEMPHIS . . . PLANTER'S HOUSE ON

THE MISSISSIPPI . . . STEAMER WOODING

UP . . . COTTON BLOCKADE . . . MERIDIAN

. . . LOUISIANA SUGAR PLANTATION . . .

BATON ROUGE . . . SOUTHWEST PASS . . .

BAYOU OF THE MISSISSIPPI . . . NEW

ORLEANS . . . LEVEE SCENES . . . A

"CREVASSE" . . . NEW ORLEANS DOCKS

. . . THE BELIZE . . . CYPRESS SWAMP

. . . MOSS GATHERING

GRAND TOWER ROCK, BELOW ST. LOUIS

Down the Mississippi... from St. Louis to the Gulf

THE "MIGHTY MISSISSIPPI" REALLY begins where once it ended, in a great alluvial plain some thirty miles south of St. Louis, and over a thousand miles from its source. For it is here that the river, fed by the Missouri, Illinois, and Ohio, becomes the muddied, surging Mississippi of song and story.

Just as the New World had once beckoned immigrants from a crowded and exhausted Europe, so the Lower Mississippi valley offered its rich, dark soil to planters from the East. Intensive cultivation had worn out much of the Eastern cotton and tobacco lands, and productive land was growing scarce. But in the Lower Mississippi valley, men could dream once again of boundless riches. And for roughly half a century the dreams came true. England and America clamored for cotton. By the 1830s the seemingly inexhaustible soil of the Lower Mississippi valley and the easy access to the port of New Orleans offered by the river itself drew pioneers westward.

Travelers along the river in those years could see broad cotton fields stretching out beyond the riverbanks and, farther in the distance, the stately homes of the great planters. Closer to shore, they could see the wretched huts of the Mississippi woodcutters and squatters, and everywhere they could see the slaves.

The wealth of the Mississippi valley was indeed prodigious, but the river has always held claim against those who farmed its valley. Disastrous floods often took back all that the river had given, and more. So, from Illinois to the Gulf, great levees were built, in the endless struggle with the river.

Planters and slaves, roustabouts and dandies, riverboat gamblers and langorous belles thronged the streets of thriving river towns. The lore of the steamboats anchored in these towns excited generations of young boys, who dreamed of the romantic and often treacherous voyages up and down the river.

Cape Girardeau, in Illinois, may be considered the real gateway to the Lower Mississippi. It is here that the river has swollen to its full strength and the great levees begin. Downstream in Illinois lies Cairo, the staging area for the Union's forces in their conquest of the river. Farther south, in Tennessee, is Memphis, once cotton capital of the Lower Mississippi, and home to both Davy Crockett and W. C. Handy. It was just below Memphis that Hernando de Soto and his party first saw the Mississippi in 1541.

Arkansas's Helena, and Mississippi's Greenville and Vicksburg all shared as well in its destruction. Natchez, however, shared only the wealth. Unharmed by Union fire, Natchez retained its elegant antebellum homes and still remains a living monument to Southern culture before the Civil War. Indeed, no traveler along the river has failed to remark on the beauty of Natchez: situated high on a bluff at a bend in the river, its sloping streets are lined with gracious homes built more than a century ago.

As the river reached Baton Rouge it enters flatlands, where it spreads out into innumerable bayous and begins its final, three-pronged journey to the Gulf. Here at Baton Rouge, founded by the French in their earliest explorations of the river, moss, cane, and live oak, redolent of the town's quieter past, exist along with the throbbing machinery of the nation's largest oil refinery.

Below Baton Rouge the Mississippi flows through the gloomy bayous, swamps, cypress groves, and hanging moss of southern Louisiana, until it finally reaches New Orleans. Founded by Bienville in 1718, on orders from France, it was ceded to the United States in 1803 as part of the Louisiana Purchase. New Orleans, though renowned as French, has an architecture more unique to Spain. In 1788 much of the old wooden part of the town burnt and was replaced by the Spanish-style brick and plaster buildings which constitute the Vieux Carré.

Into New Orleans, and out again through its great port, poured the riches of the Mississippi: cotton, surely, but also corn, wheat, meat, fruit, and sugar. Its air of a gracious, somewhat quaint "ville de province"—as Mrs. Trollope remembered it—belie the tougher nature of this great port city, in which stevedores, boatmen, and pirates clustered, along with more genteel inhabitants. And here in New Orleans "Ol' Man River," silent witness of so much history, finally ends his long journey, as his mighty, brown waters pour slowly into the Gulf.

The levees along the St. Louis banks—jammed with hundreds of steamboats: from faraway Pittsburgh to the east; St. Paul to the north; New Orleans downriver, gateway to the Gulf and the seas . . . .

At the crossroads of the Mississippi system St. Louis was able to levy a toll on the river trade in all directions. After the *Yellowstone's* pioneering trip up the Missouri in 1823, steamboats poked ever farther into the back country until in 1859 one vessel came within fifteen miles of Fort Benton, three thousand five hundred and sixty miles from the sea. Furs from the Northwest, annuities to the Indians, Mormon exiles, military personnel and supplies, emigrants, gold seekers— first California bound, then for Montana—all found space on the Missouri River boats; and St. Louis was the terminal of the traffic. Manufactures, hogs, grain, and other produce arrived from Ohio and Illinois river ports for transshipment. "All these advantages combine to make [St. Louis] a place of great trade," wrote F.B. Mayer in 1851. "It's inhabitants . . . all wear the anxious & care worn looks of 'men of business.' " Almost always, Mayer added, nearly one hundred steamboats could be counted on the levee, "taking in and discharging freight, letting off steam, & pushing out or arriving . . . .

ST. LOUIS ON THE MISSISSIPPI

MARINE HOSPITAL, ST. LOUIS

*. . . pulsing with the heartbeat of the growing nation—
a scene of hectic activity—"for two miles a forest
of smokestacks . . . a dense mass of confusion and bustle"*

THE LEVEE OR LANDING, ST. LOUIS

There is probably no busier scene in America in the same space. For two miles a forest of smoke stacks is seen towering above the 'arks' from which they seem to grow. All between this and the line of warehouses is filled with a dense mass of apparently inextricable confusion & bustle, noise & animation. More steamboats are probably seen here than at any port in the world . . . ."

MARSHALL B. DAVIDSON
Life in America, 1951

THE LEVEE AT ST. LOUIS

Midway along the length of the Mississippi—at its confluence with the Missouri, the thriving port of St. Louis grew as the great thoroughfare of western migration . . .

The appearance of St. Louis was not calculated to make a favorable impression upon the first visit, with its long dirty and quicksand beach, numbers of long, empty keelboats tied to stakes driven in the sand, squads of idle boatmen passing to and fro, here and there numbers pitching quoits; others running foot races, rough and tumble fights; and shooting at a target was one of their occupations while in port.

JAMES HEALEY WHITE

Early Days in St. Louis, 1819

LOCUST STREET, ST. LOUIS

By the mid-century there were probably a thousand boats operating regularly on the Mississippi. Even at the beginning of our period, in 1834, the steam tonnage on that river—39,000—was nearly half that of the whole British Empire, and it multiplied sixfold in sixteen years. Over the unknown spot where De Soto had been given his watery grave in the midst of a continental wilderness, there now raced against each other great boats, gleaming with lights at night, costing a hundred thousand dollars and more, carrying their picturesque hundred or two of passengers—gamblers, merchants, slaves and immigrants, fur traders, cotton planters, every imaginable type of humanity—and cargoes of every sort of merchandise. Of accidents there were plenty. Even when the fires were not being fed with resin or oil-soaked wood, while safety valves were illegally fastened down, in the races between steamers which were a favorite form of river sport, the snags, sand bars, explosions, and sudden conflagrations of the flimsy superstructures often resulted in heavy loss of life.

JAMES TRUSLOW ADAMS

Epic of America, 1933

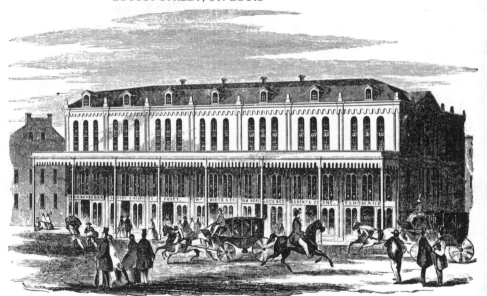

VERANDA ROW, ST. LOUIS

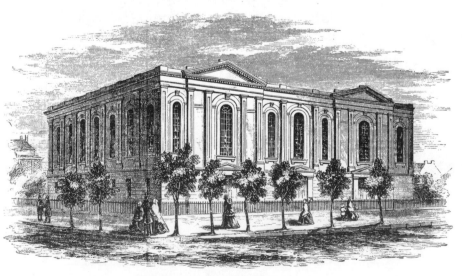

MEDICAL DEPARTMENT, ST. LOUIS

. . . where, in earlier days, emigrants and traders—in an endless caravan of wagons and coaches—purchased supplies for the journey west: in latter days, the hub for rail lines

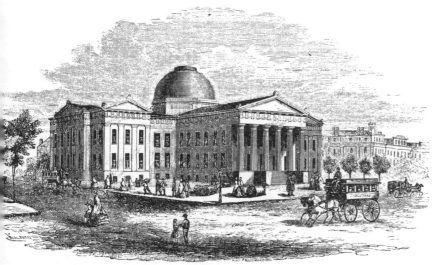

COURT HOUSE, ST. LOUIS

The cities of the West are all of them pre-eminently cosmopolitan cities. The Germans have their quarters there—sometimes half the city, their newspapers, and their clubs; the Irish have theirs; and the French theirs. The Mississippi River is the great cosmopolitan which unites all people, which gives a definite purpose of their activity, and determines their abode, and which enables the life of every one, the inhabitants themselves and their products, to circulate from the one end to the other of this great central valley.

FREDRIKA BREMER
America of the Fifties, 1933

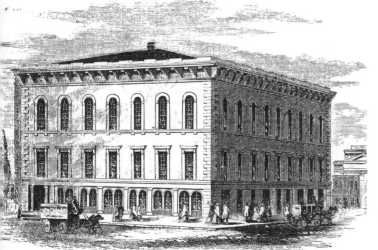

MERCANTILE LIBRARY, ST. LOUIS

BIDDLE MARKET, ST. LOUIS

ST. CHARLES RAILROAD BRIDGE, MISSOURI

When—between 1867 and 1874—James Eads threw his giant bridge across the Mississippi, Mark Twain predicted "the beginning of the end of the great age of steamboat navigation on the river"

As different railroads converged on the Mississippi and Missouri Rivers to take off across the rest of the continent, bridges sprang up to expedite the East-West traffic flow. The bridge at St. Louis, built by James B. Eads between 1867 and 1874, was the most costly and important of the early ones. Carriages and railroads traveled on separate levels sixty feet above the water. Revisiting St. Louis after the bridge had been built Mark Twain reviewed the melancholy and woeful sight of a half-dozen "sound-asleep steamboats" where once there had been a mile of wide-awake ones. "Remains of former steamboatmen told me," he wrote, " . . .that the bridge doesn't pay. Still, it can be no sufficient compensation to a corpse to know that the dynamite that laid him out was not as good quality as it had been supposed to be." Steamboating as Mark Twain remembered it was all but dead.

MARSHALL B. DAVIDSON
Life in America, 1951

5th St. near the Barracks

New Court House

Lafayette Park

St. Louis

Olive St.

On Chestnut St.

A nook in McDowell's College

On Chouteau Avenue.

On the Fair Ground

ST. LOUIS

But what may have been lost in river traffic was more than compensated for in other directions, as buildings and institutions sprang up, at a great rate, in St. Louis

SCENES IN ST. LOUIS

St. Louis is ordained by the decrees of physical nature to become the great inland metropolis of this continent. It cannot escape the magnificence of its destiny. Greatness is the necessity of its position. New York may be the head, but St. Louis will be the heart of America. The stream of traffic which must flow through this mart will enrich it with alluvial deposits of gold. Its central location and facilities of communication unmistakably indicate the leading part which this city will take in the exchange and distribution of the products of the Mississippi Valley . . . . It is the geographical centre of a valley which embraces 1,200,000 square miles. In its course of 3,200 miles, the Mississippi borders on Missouri 470 miles. Of the 3,000 miles of the Missouri, 500 lie within the limits of our own State. St. Louis is mistress of more than 16,500 miles of river navigation. This metropolis, though in the infancy of its greatness, is already a large city. Its length is about eight miles, and its width three. Suburban residences, the outposts of the grand advance, are now stationed six or seven miles from the river.

ANSELM L. STRAUSS, ED.
The American City, 1968

*Inland lifeline of the nation—highway for trade and travel
—the river gave birth to a hundred towns and cities in ten
states—some tiny hamlets, others giant sprawling cities*

Mississippi begins in the lobby of a Memphis, Tennessee, hotel and extends south to the Gulf of Mexico. It is dotted with little towns concentric about the ghosts of the horses and mules once tethered to the hitch-rail enclosing the county courthouse and it might almost be said to have only two directions, north and south, since until a few years ago it was impossible to travel east or west in it unless you walked or rode one of the horses or mules. Even in the boy's early manhood, to reach by rail either of the adjacent county towns thirty miles away to the east or west, you had to travel ninety miles in three different directions on three different railroads. In the beginning it was virgin—to the west, along the Big River, the alluvial swamps threaded by black, almost motionless bayous and impenetrable with cane and buckvine and cypress and ash and oak and gum; to the east, the hardwood ridges and the prairies where the Appalachian Mountains died and buffalo grazed; to the south, the pine barrens and the moss-hung live oaks and the greater swamps, less of earth than water and lurking with alligators and water moccasins, where Louisiana in its time would begin.

WILLIAM FAULKNER
American Panorama, 1947

VICKSBURG, MISSISSIPPI

MEMPHIS, MISSISSIPPI

Along its banks lay virgin forests, alluvial swamps, quiet bayous, prairies of grazing buffalo—plantation homes in Louisiana and Mississippi built upon cotton and sugar profits

PLANTER'S HOUSE AND SUGAR PLANTATION, ON THE MISSISSIPPI

The whole of the steamboats of which you have an account did not perform voyages to New Orleans only, but to all points on the Mississippi, and other rivers which fall into it. I am certain that since the above date the number has increased, but to what extent I cannot at present say. When steamboats first plied between Shippingport and New Orleans, the cabin passage was a hundred dollars, and a hundred and fifty dollars on the upward voyage. In 1829, I went down to Natchez from Shippingport for twenty-five dollars, and ascended from New Orleans on board the Philadelphia, in the beginning of January 1830, for sixty dollars, having taken two state-rooms for my wife and myself. On that voyage we met with a trifling accident, which protracted it to fourteen days; the computed distance being, as mentioned above, 1650 miles, although the real distance is probably less. I do not remember to have spent a day without meeting with a steam-boat, and some days we met several. I might here be tempted to give you a description of one of these steamers of the western waters, but the picture having been often drawn by abler hands, I shall desist.

JOHN JAMES AUDUBON
American Scenery and Character, 1926

PLANTER'S HOUSE ON THE MISSISSIPPI

At many points along the snakelike course of the Mississippi, heavily laden steamboats on the river— at one time estimated to be well in the thousands . . .

Indeed there are solitary cabins of wood-cutters, who fix their dwellings on piles or blocks, raised above the inundation, who stay there to supply the steamboats with wood. In effect, to visit this very portion of the river in the autumn after the subsiding of the spring-floods, to see its dry banks, its clean sand-bars, and all traces of inundation gone, except its marks upon the trunks of the trees, one would have no suspicion of the existence of such swamp and overflow as it now exhibits.

TIMOTHY FLINT
Recollections of the Last Ten Years, 1826

I suppose that St. Louis and New Orleans have not suffered materially by the change, but alas for the wood-yard man! He used to fringe the river all the way; his close-ranked merchandise stretched from the one city to the other, along the banks, and he sold uncountable cords of it every year for cash on the nail; but all the scattering boats that are left burn coal now and the seldomest spectacle on the Mississippi to-day is a woodpile. Where now is the one wood-yard man.

MARK TWAIN
Life on the Mississippi, 1874

STEAMER WOODING UP ON THE MISSISSIPPI

. . . Their high-pressure engines—gluttons for fuel—burning daily as much as thirty cords of wood, had to restock at least twice a day at wooding stations along the riverbanks

Negroes along the rivers are gorgeous romancers. They are full of stories of catfish as big as whales, of enormous snakes, and of incredible treasure finds. To the latter many look hopefully forward for the solution of all their difficulties in life. They put up with a miserable muddy existence year after year in the hope that floodwaters may bring some great prize which will enable them to satisfy all of their dreams. "Ole Man River" is for the colored children of his banks very much the measure of all things—he is fate, hope, and tragedy all in one. The most desirable job a river Negro can obtain is one on a boat which will take him to and from such legendary and inspiring river places as Cincinnati, St. Louis, Memphis, or New Orleans. The cook of a towboat on which I journeyed from Cairo to New Orleans was so proud of his position and his view of himself as a much traveled man that he could even speak of the sporty children of Beale Street as "dem niggahs." His lips curled scornfully about the "shiftless no-'count niggahs," who lived on the riverbanks waiting for flood riches and who "nevah got nuthin' but a mess o' catfish and a han'ful of ole boards."

THOMAS HART BENTON
An Artist in America, 1937

Throughout the vast regions of the South—where King Cotton reigned—the daily life of master and slave, the plantation system, and its effect, as an institution, on human freedom . . .

There were two other large plantations near him, in both of which the negroes were turned out to work at half-past three every morning—I might hear the bell ring for them —and frequently they were not stopped till nine o'clock at night, Saturday nights the same as any other. One of them belonged to a very religious lady, and on Sunday mornings at half-past nine she had her bell rung for Sunday school, and after Sunday school they had a meeting, and after dinner another religious service. Every negro on the plantation was obliged to attend all these exercises, and if they were not dressed clean they were whipped. They were never allowed to go off the plantation, and if they were caught speaking to a negro from any other place, they were whipped. They could all of them repeat the catechism, he believed, but they were the dullest, and laziest, and most sorrowful negroes he ever saw.

FREDERICK LAW OLMSTED

Seaboard Slave States, 1856

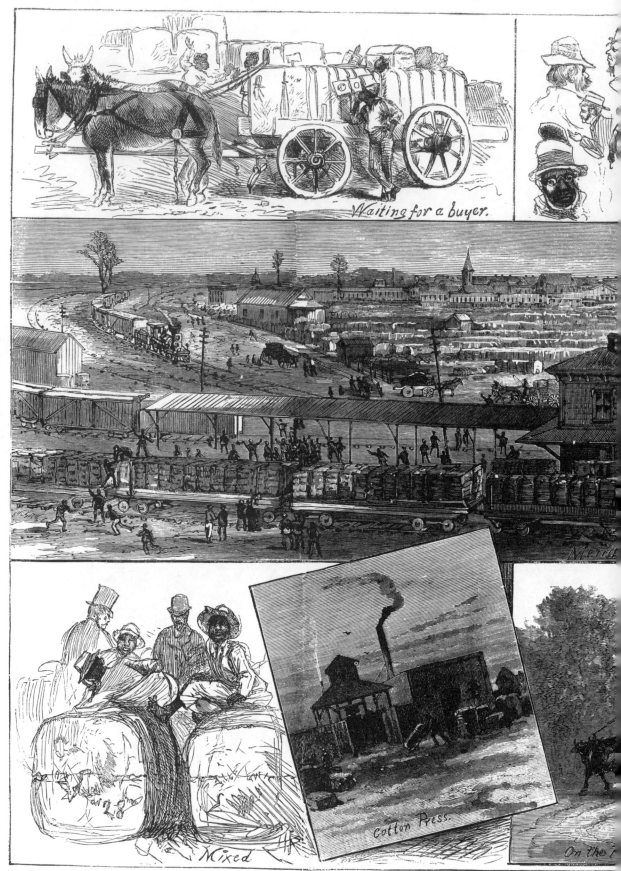

COTTON BLOCKADE, AT MERIDIAN, MISSISSIPPI

. . . varied little from state to state. In the days before improved agricultural equipment, the disgruntled labor force protested, setting up a blockade of rail shipments

But what words shall describe the Mississippi, great father of rivers, who (praise be to Heaven) has no young children like him! An enormous ditch, sometimes two or three miles wide, running liquid mud, six miles an hour: its strong and frothy current choked and obstructed everywhere by huge logs and whole forest trees: now twining themselves together in great rafts, from the interstices of which a sedgy lazy foam works up, to float upon the water's top; now rolling past like monstrous bodies, their tangled roots showing like matted hair; now glancing singly by like giant leeches; and now writhing round and round in the vortex of some small whirlpool, like wounded snakes. The banks low, the trees dwarfish, the marshes swarming with frogs, the wretched cabins few and far apart, their inmates hollow-cheeked and pale, the weather very hot, mosquitoes penetrating into every crack and crevice of the boat, mud and slime on everything: nothing pleasant in its aspect, but the harmless lightning which flickers every night upon the dark horizon.

CHARLES DICKENS
American Notes, 1842

Typical of the great gentlemen of the lower South was John Hampden Randolph, who, in 1841 purchased a plantation in Iberville Parish, Louisiana—turning from cotton to sugar

In the moist, hot climate of the lower Mississippi sugar cane flourishes. What cotton has been to Alabama, sugar has been to Louisiana. Very early sugar mills appeared and sugar plantations were laid out. Neither the institution of slavery nor the plantation system required essential modification to fit the requirements of the crop. The pictures drawn herewith well represent the conditions of the old slave days, the drove of slaves—both men and women—the ubiquitous mules teams and carts, the broad open spaces, the simple mill and equipment for crushing and boiling, and the planter's house.

The Pageant of America, 1926

A LOUISIANA SUGAR PLANTATION

His land holdings increased to several thousand acres—his labor force from 23 to 195 slaves—becoming more profitable after the Civil War, as free Negro labor became available

A Sugar Cane Field

A Field Hand

The Planters House

White cotton fields and sugar plantations pushed westward into the black belt of Alabama, the lowlands of Mississippi and Louisiana, and on into the broad warm plains of Texas. With them went the negro and the plantation system. The new soil was fertile, cotton and sugar were profitable and labor scarce. Slavery which had seemed on the decline in the late eighteenth century sprang into new life. Even the ideal of aristocracy which had wavered in Jefferson's day was steadied by triumphant cotton and the expansion of negro slavery. Civilization in the heart of the South was based upon agriculture, and the planters, in the midst of smaller landholders, became a cultivated gentry worthy of the best traditions of aristocratic England. In their fine old homes moved a society out of which the crudities of the New World had been refined while much of its strength had been preserved. With dignity and courtesy they ruled the affairs of their local communities. How different from the horny-handed folk north of the Ohio!

The Pageant of America, 1926

*Over two hundred miles upriver from New Orleans,
Baton Rouge—since 1849 the capital of Louisiana—its
deep-water port a rail hub and center of industrial activity*

Baton Rouge, capital and third largest city of Louisiana, overlooks the Mississippi River from Istrouma Bluff. It is a modern city bordered by great industrial plants and by tree-shaded reaches of the Capitol grounds. Residential streets are lined with oaks, elms, and magnolias. Here in 1719 the French built a fort to subdue the Indian tribes and gave it the name ("Istrouma" meaning "red stick" or in French, "baton rouge") derived from the reddened post that stood here to indicate the boundary between lands of two different tribes. Settlement was transferred, in 1763, along with other Louisiana territory ceded by the Treaty of Paris, to Great Britain, which made the port a point of origin for contraband commerce with Spanish Louisiana. During the American Revolution, the British garrison was defeated and forced to withdraw by the forces of Don Bernardo de Galvez, Spanish Governor of Louisiana, at the First Battle of Baton Rouge, September 21, 1779. The city remained under Spanish rule until American-born residents of the surrounding parishes rebelled and captured the fort—also the settlement that had grown around it—at the Second Battle of Baton Rouge, September 23, 1810. They raised the "Bonnie Blue Flag" of the West Florida Republic. In 1817 the town of Baton Rouge was incorporated and in 1849 it became the capital city.

The American Guide, 1949

BATON ROUGE, ON THE MISSISSIPPI

UNLOADING MILITARY STORES, BATON ROUGE LEVEE

Settled by "Cajuns"—Acadians who emigrated from French-Canada generations ago—the bayou country is formed of extensive lowlands bordering the Mississippi delta area

SOUTHWEST PASS

For miles before you reach the passes, you observe the muddy Mississippi water in great masses, rolling and tumbling unmingled with the briny blue sea. Gradually the dull hue assumes supremacy, and at last you are greeted by a simple object of beauty and practical interest, which has been erected by human hands. Rising up from the interminable level is a solitary light-house, built at the entrance of the Southwest Pass. This structure is the sentinel on guard—an immovable point, from the bearings of which the pilot is enabled to bring his ship to safe harbor. Just inside the Northeast Pass is a huge mud-bank, known as the Balize. Long years ago people, mostly of Spanish origin, who found it irksome to live under the restraints of settled communities, made a home at the Balize, tempted by the isolation, the abundance of game, and the occasional reward for acting as pilots or wreckers. Within a half century the growing demands of commerce have changed the rude huts of the settlement into pleasant residences.

T. B. THORPE

Picturesque America, 1872

A BAYOU OF THE MISSISSIPPI

*Black smoke belching from twin stacks of riverboats—
flags flying at jack staff—gang planks in the ready position
as passengers, heavily laden, scampered aboard*

It was always the custom for the boats to leave New Orleans between four and five o'clock in the afternoon. From three o'clock onward they would be burning rosin and pitchpine (the sign of preparation), and so one had the picturesque spectacle of a rank, some two or three miles long, of tall, ascending columns of coal-black smoke; a colonnade which supported a sable roof of the same smoke blended together and spreading abroad over the city. Every outward-bound boat had its flag flying at the jackstaff, and sometimes a duplicate on the verge-staff astern. Two or three miles of mates were commanding and swearing with more than usual emphasis: countless processions of freight barrels and boxes were spinning, athwart the levee and flying abroad the stage-planks; belated passengers were dodging and skipping among these frantic things, hoping to reach the forecastle companionway alive, but having their doubts about it; women with reticules and bandboxes were trying to keep up with husbands freighted with carpet sacks and crying babies, and making a failure of it by losing their heads in the whirl and roar and general distraction; drays and baggage-vans were clattering hither and thither in a wild hurry, every now and then getting blocked and jammed together, and then . . .

ARRIVALS AT THE LEVEE, NEW ORLEANS

Such was the scene of helter-skelter confusion with every steamboat's departure—the chaos and turmoil reaching a crescendo of excitement as "last bells" clanged their final warning

LEVEE AT JACKSON SQUARE, NEW ORLEANS

COTTON BALES AND COTTON PRESS, NEW ORLEANS

. . . during ten seconds one could not see them for the profanity, except vaguely and dimly; every windlass connected with every forehatch from one end of that long array of steamboats to the other, was keeping up a deafening whizz and whir, lowering freight into the hold, and the half-naked crews of perspiring Negroes that worked them were roaring such songs as "De Las' Sack! De Las' Sack!"—inspired to unimaginable exaltation by the chaos of turmoil and racket that was driving everybody else mad. By this time the hurricane and boiler decks of the steamers would be packed black with passengers. The "last bells" would begin to clang, all down the line, and then the powwow seemed to double; in a moment or two the final warning came—a simultaneous din of Chinese gongs, with the cry, "All dat ain't goin', please to git asho'!"—and behold the powwow quadrupled! People came swarming ashore, overturning excited stragglers that were trying to swarm aboard. One more moment later a long array of stage-planks was being hauled in, each with its customary latest passenger clinging to the end of it with teeth, nails, and everything else, and the customary latest procrastinator making a wild spring shoreward over his head.

MARK TWAIN
The Gilded Age, 1873

Wharves of the Queen City of the South are lined with a congeries of keelboats, barges, river steamboats jostling with ocean-going schooners, five abreast at quayside

One hundred miles from the mouth of the Mississippi, and something more than a thousand from the mouth of the Ohio, just below a sharp point of the river is situated on its east bank, the city of New Orleans, the great commercial capital of the Mississippi valley. The position for a commercial city is unrivalled, I believe, by any one in the world. At a proper distance from the Gulf of Mexico,—on the banks of a stream which may be said almost to water a world,—but a little distance from Lake Ponchartrain, and connected with it by a navigable canal,—the immense alluvion contiguous to it—penetrated in all directions either by *Bayous* formed by nature, or canals which cost little more trouble in the making, than ditches, —steamboats visiting it from fifty different shores, —possessing the immediate agriculture of its own state, the richest in America, and as rich as any in the world, with the continually increasing agriculture of the upper country, its position far surpasses that of New York itself. It has one dreary drawback—the insalubrity of its situation. Could the immense swamps between it and the bluffs be drained, and the improvements commenced in the city completed; in short, could its atmosphere ever become a dry one, it would soon leave the greatest cities of the Union behind.

TIMOTHY FLINT
*Recollections of the
Last Ten Years, 1826*

THE MISSISSIPPI AT NEW ORLEANS

A "CREVASSE" ON THE MISSISSIPPI

From New Orleans to the delta . . . low-lying banks, sandbars, and marshes mark the channel to the sea—ideal habitat for migratory wildfowl—before reaching South Pass and the Gulf

TOWING ON THE MISSISSIPPI, FROM BELIZE TO NEW ORLEANS

THE BELIZE, MOUTH OF THE MISSISSIPPI

That trip we went to Grand Gulf, from New Orleans, in four days (three hundred and forty miles); the *Eclipse* and *Shotwell* did it in one. We were nine days out, in the chute of 63 (seven hundred miles); the *Eclipse* and *Shotwell* went there in two days. Something over a generation ago, a boat called the *J.M. White* went from New Orleans to Cairo in three days, six hours, and forty-four minutes. In 1853 the *Eclipse* made the same trip in three days, three hours, and twenty minutes. In 1870 the *R.E. Lee* did it in three days and *one* hour. This last is called the fastest trip on record. I will try to show that it was not. For this reason: the distance between New Orleans and Cairo, when the *J.M. White* ran it, was about eleven hundred and six miles; consequently her average speed was a trifle over fourteen miles per hour. In the *Eclipse's* day the distance between the two ports had become reduced to one thousand and eighty miles; consequently her average speed was a shade under fourteen and three-eights miles per hour. In the *R.E. Lee's* time the distance had diminished to about one thousand and thirty miles; consequently her average was about fourteen and one-eighth miles per hour. Therefore the *Eclipse's* was conspicuously the fastest time that has ever been made.

MARK TWAIN

Life on the Mississippi, 1874

The lush, semitropical climate of Louisiana—especially in its flooded swamplands—produces luxuriant forests where cypress trees and Spanish moss flourish

The first grand tree-development of the "swamps" is the tall and ghostly cypress. It flourishes in our semi-tropical climate of the South, being nourished by warmth, water, and the richest possible soil. The Louisiana product finds a rival in Florida; and in both places this remarkable tree is perfect in growth, often reaching the height of one hundred and thirty feet. The base of the trunk, generally covered with ooze and mud, conceals the formidable "spikes," called "knees," which spring up from the roots. These excrescences, when young, are sharp and formidable weapons, and, young or old, are nearly as hard as steel. To travel in safety through a flooded cypress-swamp on horseback, the greatest care must be taken to avoid the concealed cypress-knees; for, if your generous steed, while floundering in the soft mud, settles down upon one of them, he may never recover from the injury. The bark of the tree is spongy and fibrous; and the trunk of the tree oftens attains fifty or sixty feet without a branch. The foliage, as seen from below, is as soft as green silken fringe, and strangely beautiful and delicate, when contrasted with the tree itself and the gloomy, repulsive place of its nativity. The wood, though light and soft, is of extraordinary durability. It has been asserted, that cypress-trees which have been buried a thousand years under the solid but always damp earth, now retain every quality of the most perfect wood. At the root of the cypress the palmetto flourishes in vigor; and its intensely green spear-like foliage adds to the variety of the vegetable productions in the forest solitudes.

T. B. THORPE
Picturesque America 1872

CYPRESS SWAMP

Comparatively within a few years, the Spanish moss has become important as an article of commerce, for, when plucked from the trees, from which it is easily separated, and then thoroughly "cured" and threshed of its delicate integuments of bark and leaves, it is found that though the long, thready moss is a delicate fibre as black as jet, and almost as thick as horsehair, which it strikingly resembles. For the stuffing of mattresses and cushions it is valuable, and the increasing demand for it has already opened a new field of enterprise among the denizens of the swamp.

T. B. THORP
Picturesque America, 187.

MOSS GATHERING

List of Authors

Acknowledgments

The American Guide. Copyright 1977. By permission of Hastings House Publishers.

Stephen Vincent Benet. "John Brown's Body" from *Selected Works of Stephen Vincent Benet*. Published by Holt, Rinehart & Winston Inc. 1927, 1928 by Stephen Vincent Benet. Copyright renewed 1955 by Rosemary Carr Benet. Reprinted by permission of Brandt & Brandt Literacy Agency.

Stars Fell on Alabama. Copyright 1934 by Carl Carmer. Reprinted by permission of the state.

Marshall B. Davidson. *Life in America*. Copyright 1951 by Marshall B. Davidson. Reprinted by permission of Houghton Mifflin Company.

Arnold Ehrlich (ed). *The Beautiful Country*. Copyright 1970 by the Viking Press Inc. Reprinted by permission of the Viking Press, Inc.

William Francis Guess. *South Carolina*. Copyright 1947.

John Gunther. *Inside U.S.A.* Copyright 1946, 1947 by John Gunther. Copyright 1947 by the Curtis Publishing Company. Reprinted by permission of Harper and Row Publishers, Inc.

Walter Havighurst. *Land of the Long Horizons*. Copyright 1960 by Walter Havighurst. Reprinted by permission of Coward, McCann and Geoghegan, Inc.

Ohio, A Bicentennial History. Copyright 1976 by American Association for State and Local History. Reprinted by permission of W.W. Norton & Company Inc.

Harnett T. Kane. *Gone are the Days: An Illustrated History of the Old South*. Copyright 1960 by Harnett T. Kane. Reprinted by permission of the publishers, E.P. Dutton & Co., Inc.

Samuel E. Morison. *The Oxford History of the American People*. Copyright 1965 by Samuel Eliot Morison. Reprinted by permission Curtis Brown, Ltd.

William T. Polk. *Southern Accent*. Copyright 1953. Reprinted by permission of William Morrow & Co., Inc.

Notes

Notes

Notes